LIFE'S LESSONS,
prn

Examination of One Doctor's Journey

Paul M. Gustman MD

ISBN-13: 9781514122211

Title: Life's Lessons, prn

Author: Paul M. Gustman MD
ISBN: 1514122219
Library of Congress Control Number: 2015915645
CreateSpace Independent Publishing Platform
North Charleston, South Carolina

WRITE? ... RIGHT!

I awaken in the morning with an understanding, a convergence of ideas that occurred while I slept. There is a compulsion to write it down, to expand upon the idea, to show its relevance to bigger issues.

And so I write.

The great fear of aging is loss: of autonomy, of bodily function and most of all loss of the person we were. We fear being forgotten by those who succeed us. We fear not sharing the wisdom accumulated in seventy years causing the young to repeat our mistakes. I wonder if I have not been clear in creating a moral framework for my family, or showing their limitless potential, or telling of my love and faith in them.

And so I write.

Writing is a way to deal with knotty issues, sometimes of the present, more often of the past—unresolved though ever-present through the decades, a stone in the shoe or a bolder in life's path.

But on paper the issues cannot be avoided. Like a debate with oneself, each point must be evaluated, placed in its hierarchy of importance. Events from the past are explored by a person who has now seen more, has learned what the stresses of life can do, and at a time when the hurt throbs less. In the analysis lies a kernel of understanding, the first step of healing.

And so I write.

Writing brings joy to me and those close enough to share my experiences or feelings. If a story takes the reader inside a factory, or on safari, or shares the insecurities of a doctor in training, then I have done my job. If I have relayed to my friends what their friendship has meant over the years causing a few tears to be shed by all, then I know that a basic truth has been revealed. I build with words a picture of my life and thoughts.

The keyboard is my hammer and saw. Like a well mitered corner, the keystrokes produce a deep sense of satisfaction.

And so I write.

"The essayist is the self-liberated man, sustained by the childish belief that everything he thinks about, everything that happens to him, is of general interest."
The Essayist and the Essay   by E.B. White

"To be a writer is a monstrously arrogant act."
To Show and to Tell   by Phillip Lopate

"Memory is never a precise duplicate of the original; it is a continuing act of creation."
The Boston Globe   by Rosalind Cartwright,
                               Sleep Researcher

ACKNOWLEDGMENTS

I would like to thank Eric Selby, the Chief of the Editorial Police. His endless encouragement and good cheer have resulted in the completion of this book.

Thanks also to Lisa Reyes, my first writing instructor. Her thoughtful analysis, inspiration and specific suggestions led to another course, and another, and another.

Thanks to Noah Scheiner, our resident artist, for creating the book cover.

Thank you to my first, middle and last editor, my cheerleader and partner in this great, forty-nine year adventure—my wife, my love, Marilyn. There are not enough pages to express my gratitude.

Thanks to my two children and their wonderful spouses who have provided me with endless joy and six fabulous grandchildren, for whom this book has been written.

INDEX

FAMILY

FATHERS AND SONS

As the middle child my path was already established. My brother, a year and nine days my senior, pushed the boundaries, confronted when necessary and left for the safety of my aunt's house when conditions were unbearable. His victories were my inheritance. For me avoiding conflict was always the easier path. My brother made that possible and for that I can forgive the myriad of peculiarities that made him a challenging roommate. The price for being in the vanguard was unhappiness. He says his life began when he left home and married. He never once lifted a hand in anger to his children. When raising his own son he would express extreme frustration or anger by biting his own knuckle. He says he can still see the tooth marks forty years later.

My sister, two years younger, faced her own obstacles growing up. She had a difficult father and a dominant older brother. It was a rare family picture where she was not crying. She learned to fight back. In one defining evening when parents weren't home, my brother picked on her and crossed an invisible line of tolerability. There was, in our living room, a beautiful and substantial metal fruit bowl with a rounded bottom, the sides of which were joined by the gentle arc of a thick metal handle. She swung it using wrist and centrifugal force to create maximal acceleration. I recall the sound of that bowl colliding with my brother's head. It caused no permanent injury. But she was treated differently thereafter.

She had the additional burden of growing up female in a household where income barely covered necessities. She was expected to go to work after high school and "help support the boys" while they got an education which would allow them, in turn, to support their families. A proto-feminist, this did not sit well with her on many levels. In later years she told me of conflict lasting almost a year before my father was worn down by her persistence and the help of our relatives before she was allowed to attend college. She has lived her life on the fringes of protest, first in the Peace Corps then various Zen centers and communes. Most of her life's work has been setting up programs in the state of Washington to improve infant nutrition and the lives of seniors. She has by choice had no children.

I was the good child. I never believed my brother and sister when they said I was treated differently. I discovered letters from my father in my mother's papers after her death which validated their view. I was the good student, the one who didn't give trouble, the one who listened. I'm not sure if that was a survival mechanism or merely the path of least resistance, the space unoccupied. I was surely aware of my father's temper. Displeasing him was something you did at your own peril. Good news was expected to be shared. Praise would follow. Sharing of daily events was not something I recall.

My father was the oldest of four. Having immigrant parents, he grew up in a poor section of lower Manhattan. Fighting was an integral part of life and by all accounts he excelled at it. Though only five-foot-six he responded quickly to any real or perceived insult. He was the protector of his two younger brothers and only sister. His younger brother's goal growing up was to be "a tough guy like Sammy." In my mid teens he could lift me off the ground with one arm. His handshake left marks. Like many who had little he learned to gamble, always chasing the elusive jackpot. The horse track was his venue of choice. This habit sadly followed him all his days. My mother would be distressed to hear from a neighbor or relative that Sam was spotted at the track. Most often that meant cash shortage, conflict with the landlord when no rent money materialized and no luxuries such as toothpaste until the next month's payments came for his shellac and paint sales. This cycle twice led to our family spending a summer with Virginia relatives when groceries became unaffordable. He was his own boss and a more benevolent boss he could not have desired. His work day was most often no more than four hours which frequently included a movie.

My own relationship with my father was complex. I loved him. We would sit side by side watching TV. He loved boxing and would bob and weave along with the fighters while giving a constant running commentary: "Watch the right! Keep your guard up!" Sometimes between rounds we would surprise him and mop his sweaty brow with a wet sponge. He would laugh loudly and long.

He taught me to read the liberal columnists of the day. The *New York Post* op-ed pieces by Max Frankel or Max Lerner were not to be missed. He had always wanted to be a journalist but lasted only one year in college. Reasons for this varied in the telling. The family needed money, he said. A lack of discipline and his own spending (gambling even then?) determined his choices according to his youngest brother.

He loved to sing and in my memory he did it well. "The Girl That I Married" was his favorite song. To this day I enjoy singing and thankfully so does my wife. Aside from humiliating my daughter when growing up

("Not in public!!!!"), singing has been one of the great pleasures of my life. I do not do it well.

My father was the outgoing salesman who was never without a joke. He would laugh loudly after telling it, making it impossible not to join in. Occasionally we would groan and then often retell the same jokes to our friends. Once he overheard the retelling, he never let us forget it, especially when we didn't show appreciation for the humor. When he died he had a list of ten punch lines on a fragment of envelope in his wallet. I recall our family trying to recreate the jokes from the punch lines and in the end laughing along with him when we were successful.

But in the midst of this hand to mouth existence there was one episode of generosity that has stayed with me. My father bought shellac from a man named Ben Gart. He had an employee in his 30's named Ricky, one of the few black men I knew growing up. In my high school years, we worked side by side on school holidays and summers making, labeling and canning shellac. He was a friendly guy with a good sense of humor who treated us teenagers as equals. My Dad liked him; they joked and got along well. One day Ricky wasn't at work and I heard he was in the hospital. I later learned he had tuberculosis and would be there for several months. This was not a union shop. There was no such thing as sick leave. Ricky had a family and without him working they were in for hard times. I remember finding out that my father had been to the hospital and had given Ricky $50, an enormous sum of money for us in the 1950's. He wasn't Ricky's employer or even a close friend. He wasn't a relative, a Jew, or even of the same race—a factor which counted a lot in the days when the Yiddish word *schwartzer* or *black one* was used freely and not in a kind way. Ricky was just another guy trying to make it and he needed help. The fact that my father had $50 with him tells me it was not a spontaneous gesture. He had planned to give the money before going. It was a considered decision to share what little we had with someone who needed it more—an extra *mitzvah* in my book.

My parent's marriage was childless for eight years. At age thirty-seven my mother had her first of three children in a four year period. In those days my father owned the Certified Paint and Shellac Company. During the World War ll years he was in a unique position to build his business since he had a government allotment of raw materials for production of a needed product. He could have enlarged his customer base, streamlined production or even opened a paint store. Instead he chose to sell the raw materials on the black market to a hairbrush company. It required no work and provided immediate gratification. He bought bedroom furniture for the growing family, pieces of which still exist in the homes of his sons. He hosted lots of family parties and was by all accounts a "big shot," always used by the relatives as an insult wrapped in a compliment.

After the war, the larger paint manufacturers decided to thin out the competition by lowering prices below cost. Those with no cash reserves like my father closed their factories and went to work selling other people's products. This career path provided all there was for a family of five. Except for the rare times when the gods of horse racing shown down upon him, there were few luxuries. I felt poor only when my chino pants were so old they would shine, a fact not unnoticed by other kids. I remember how much newspaper was needed to stuff a leaky shoe when I was too old to wear galoshes, or didn't have any. Those times were infrequent and I didn't resent my position in life. I didn't resent my father or his work habits. Growing up in Brooklyn was fun. The public school was good and there were always ten heads that would pop out at the first sound of a ball bouncing on the street. A group of friends in pre-teen years could go by bus to the Dodger's game at Ebbets Field after we had collected the requisite number of Elsie ice cream wrappers to trade for bleacher seats.

When my father was stressed we knew to avoid conflict or any interaction if possible. He would yell as a harbinger of worse, if the perceived offense did not cease immediately. He grew up in a physical world and transferred that to his version of discipline. An ignored warning was followed by hard spanking or head banging or on one horrible occasion a belt. The latter involved my brother, but I witnessed it. We all cried, he in pain, I in sympathy for imagined suffering and I suspect fear. My father's bullying was never far away.

But I never learned to hate him or to imitate him. At least I hope not. (Perhaps my own kids will have a different view of history. I leave it to them to record.) My life experience has shown that we all learn from negative examples, some adopting and some rejecting. We three were unanimous in our decision to choose a different life. We all worked hard in our varied ways. Our approach to those around was, though not devoid of temper, lacked the discipline of the streets.

I wanted to be close with my children as I suspect my father did. He once told me a story of my uncle leaving his father in Russia to immigrate to the United States after a disagreement. The father's last question to him was, "How will you remember me, for good or for evil?" My father asked me the same question. Are we all not concerned with the imprint we have left behind, our legacy? Do we not seek validation for our choices from those closest to us? One day, when I have the courage, I may ask my children this very question.

MY FATHER'S HANDS

I would look carefully at my father's hand nearest to me as it rested on the wooden swan handle of his easy chair. This was part of our game of cat and mouse where I would (always unsuccessfully) try to slap his hand before he pulled it away. I spent enough time studying my target to realize the breadth and strength of that hand, not to mention the speed that nearly always led to my striking the swan just as he pulled away. I also noticed the tiny wrinkles. Millimetric in size, they created a micro-highway between hair follicles, spanning the entire hand's width, dominating and defining the cutaneous landscape. More striking was the smoothness of my own hand inches away and ready to pounce, with not a wrinkle, unscarred by the sun and the years.

There were other indications of my father's age. He had been bald since nineteen and now the fringe and chest hair were mostly white. His waistline bulged. He needed thick wire- rimmed glasses to see further than his newspaper. Cigar smoke was reflected in the slight off- color of his teeth. But it was the hands that led me to contemplate my own aging. They became my barometer of the years. If I could avoid developing those tiny wrinkles, my ten-year-old brain opined, then I would avoid getting old.

At age twelve more hair of a darker hue appeared on my hands but smoothness persisted beneath. Those same hands a decade later sprinkled dirt mixed with tears on the pine box where my father lay. Years flowed one to the next as my own family took root and blossomed.

Then my fiftieth birthday present, my first grandchild. When I held him I was amazed to note that his entire being fit in the space from my elbow to my hand, so small, so soft, so pink and so smooth. My hand touching his was different. The marks seen so long ago on my father had with an unnoticed stealth descended upon me. How had this happened? I had watched so carefully convinced in my magical thinking that vigilance would shield me from the signs and the fact of aging. But here it was: the recognition of immutable time, softened by this gift of new life, of time beginning again. Limitless potential radiated from this tiny bundle of smoothness. Life had yet to write upon his tablet. Mine, while

I was otherwise diverted, had been inscribed. Living had made its mark; but now there was another in this world to compare his hand to mine and wonder about the future.

MY EARLIEST MEMORIES

We are at the water's edge. The unobstructed wind comes off the inlet with such force that it rocks the truck and makes me search for a place away from the streams of frozen air entering the truck's cabin. I can see the line of cars and trucks hoping to get on the next ferry, being buffeted by the brutally cold wind. I am a four year old "helper" on a trip with my father to deliver shellac to a paint store in Staten Island. My older brother is not with us in the ancient, dysfunctional panel truck that provides less than adequate shelter. Heat is a sometime thing, as is protection from the wind. The rubber gaskets that used to seal the doors and windows have long ago dried, cracked and in places broken off entirely. This relic of a vehicle most often serves its purpose with deficiencies coming to the fore at times of weather extremes. Most notable is the tendency for the wiper blades to stick when we need them the most—in a snow storm. More than once I have had to keep my hand out the window to manually propel the blades when they lack the strength to push snow out of our visual field.

Earlier in the day we had delivered the five gallon cans of shellac, each weighing upwards of forty pounds. My job was to 'help' my father carry the heavy load with both our hands side-by-side on the broad metallic handle. He bore the weight while I grunted in sympathy. The store owner was suitably impressed and invited me to come back any time. With the delivery done and money exchanged, we headed back to the ferry station.

The light fades when we reach the ferry line. All semblance of warmth disappears with the setting sun. I am cold despite my sweater and winter coat. My father gives me his scarf to wrap around my face and neck. I begin to shiver. My long curly hair is an insufficient barrier as I have forgotten my hat, a point that will be loudly discussed in days to come.

I feel my chest tightening in the familiar manner of one of my asthma attacks, mild at first like the footsteps of a stalking predator. The ferry finally arrives, and we hear the loud metallic bang as the gate strikes the shore. It takes another fifteen minutes for the cars and passengers to disembark. Loading begins and we inch forward, hoping against hope that we make this boatload because the next one will be many minutes later. I begin to hear the gentle hint of whistling with each breath that foretells worsening asthma. I try to re-breathe air through the scarf and that seems to stabilize the progressive tightening of the band around my airway. We are one of the last trucks to board before the whistle sounds, signaling the end of loading and an imminent departure. I can see the gate being lifted and secured in place by long metal rods, black with grease and residue of auto exhaust.

I try to sit as quietly as possible. This keeps my airflow and wheezing at a minimum. My father keeps reassuring me that we will be home in less than an hour. This seems like forever since I am measuring time as the number of breaths it will take to get out of the cold. I do not ask for money to deposit in one of the vending machines on shipboard. My father says "you must really be feeling lousy if you don't want candy." He feels my forehead and gets a worried look on his face.

The rest of the trip is a blur of gradually deeper breathing and a feeling that my chest is swelling with un-expelled air. The sound of twenty birds trying to escape comes from within my rib cage. My father carries me inside, a sure sign that he is worried. My mother hugs me as she places her forehead to mine then runs for the thermometer. "He didn't even have a hat? Oh my God it's 104 degrees! I'm calling the doctor." She undresses me and with deft movements gets me into pajamas. I am given pills to swallow to bring down the fever while she applies cool compresses to my forehead.

In a very short time Dr. Schorr—a tall, regal looking man—in a suit as always—arrives at my bedside. He puts his well-worn black leather bag at the foot of my bed and withdraws his stethoscope. He tries to warm the head with his palm and breath, but when the metal meets my skin it is still cold enough to make me shiver. He tells my mother to boil some water so he can sterilize his needle and syringe. *Uh oh!* I watch as he takes a sugar cube and places several drops of epinephrine which he says is the fastest way to open my airway and ease the breathing. He puts the sugar cube under my tongue and instructs me to let it melt. The sugar does little to relieve the taste, so intensely bitter I wince. Then the dreaded penicillin shot. The doctor uses forceps to remove a large glass syringe from the boiling water in the pot where my mother usually boils eggs. He then does the same with a very long, thick metal needle that he attaches to the syringe with a clockwise twist. He fills it with a densely white milky emulsion withdrawn from a rubber stopped vial. He wipes alcohol on the needle and my behind. I yell, "OW!" as the syrupy liquid exits the syringe at a snail's pace. I don't cry although I would like to, as my buttock stings with the venom of a hundred wasps. I tremble as the epinephrine is absorbed through my tongue but am grateful for the easing of the vise around my chest.

"Pneumonia triggered by an asthma attack," is the doctor's pronouncement. He says he will be back in the morning to check on me and give another antibiotic shot. I hear him just outside my bedroom door enumerating tasks for my mother. Do this for fever and that for more wheezing. To my father's chagrin, he agrees with my mother that it is not wise to go out on nights like this without a hat, but notes that asthma and cold air are the main culprits here.

The recovery is complete and uneventful. Being at home with special pampering has its advantages. But no matter how much I beg and promise to wear a hat, never again does my father take me along on a delivery to Staten Island.

ASTHMA IS THE HUNTER

As the snow leopard, it stalks
Unseen, but felt
As too large paws
Barely touch the frost.

Its presence sensed
In the night whose sleep
It penetrates,
Step by stealthy step.

The purr so softly
Predicts the coming
Strangulation, ever tighter
Blocking needed air.

The boy hides under cover.
Prey, already caught
As purring is inside
Each forced breath.

The cold air brings
The snow leopard
Banished in the mist
Of aerosol salvation.

A TRIP TO THE DENTIST

I t was a trip, not a visit. All three kids in tow, my father would take us by subway from Brooklyn to exotic midtown Manhattan. Just off Times Square on the 43ʳᵈ floor was the office of Kadish Friedman DDS, a friend of my father's. He was an affable, short, chain-smoking man who must have been in the downside of his career. Perhaps we three were enough to fill a morning because I never remember other patients being there. With no dental assistants, it was a one man show. Our visits to the candy store far outnumbered our infrequent dental visits, so each was a multi-cavity catch up.

There was no such thing as a water-cooled or high-speed drill. The word Novocain was unmentioned. Once my brother, age 4, threatened to jump from the 43ʳᵈ floor window when pain followed the assurance that "this won't hurt." We were eased into the trauma that was dentistry in the early 50s. First we would be dressed in a cloth smock held together at the neck by a shiny silver beaded chain with clips on both ends. Uncle Kay, as he was known to us, would then probe with a sharp pick at each and every dental indentation that God had not created. He did this while engaged in a constant stream of conversation with my father, with whichever of us kids owned the teeth being probed, or with no one in particular. All the while a cigarette dangled from his lower lip threatening to discharge ash at any second. Was this what the gown protected us from? In my memory the smoke smelled sweet, perhaps because I was used to it since both my parents smoked in the heyday of Lucky Strikes. There was a lot of *Hmmmmming* followed by notations on a chart, which was dominated by a picture of upper and lower teeth. Too many *Hmmmm's* or shadings on the tooth diagram portended trouble to come.

Then came the low-pitched drone that followed the movement of the drive belts which went from the base of the arm to the drill tip. With the sound came other sensory assaults. The smell was part medicinal and, as the drill heated, part friction generated fumes. When there was no pain there was the certainty that it was coming. Often pain and drill heating coincided. Our only defense was a time-out signaled by raising our hand. This was respected by Uncle Kay who would promptly stop drilling, allowing both the drill and patient to cool down. Sometimes I adopted the strategy of concentrating on the feeling instead of escaping to a gentler place. By focusing on the feeling I could dismiss it—if it didn't measure up to the really bad ones. In the mind game that is pain tolerance, this removed anticipation as a multiplier and seemed to put me in control of the pain. I could downgrade it. "You call that dental pain, ha!" Not infrequently the sugar induced erosions would number six and the process dragged on until sweat permeated the back of my shirt.

Every cloud had a silver lining and ours resided on the first floor of the same office building. It was Nedick's, which served the best hot dogs and orange soda on earth. The catch was that we had to wait two hours for the mercury laden fillings to set. In my memory we waited as uncomplaining as three kids who have had *the total dental experience* can be. Rarely in my sixty years that have followed, have I tasted anything better or savored it more. It was the balm to an otherwise painful memory.

Today, while still not volunteering to visit the dentist, the memory of Nedick's softens my resistance.

The use of Novocain also helps.

THE ROOM

U nder her bed lived monsters, barely contained. The shadows from the street confirmed that they had escaped and were on the prowl. It was the last room and the most exposed. Street noises and streaks of light filtered through the jalousie windows and gossamer curtains. Shadows played on the walls and bed invading the safe space that a bedroom should offer. Even hiding under her blanket did not banish the terror of what was just outside. The whoosh of the tires brought visions of vehicles coming to get her. Far worse were the footsteps that made it personal. This was the kidnapper, the assassin coming to snatch the unwary in the dark. He could pry open one of the windows that never seemed to completely lock. He could walk through them no matter how firmly she pulled the handle to tighten the seal. The family—two rooms away, watching TV behind closed doors—would never hear her scream.

She was determined not to be taken by surprise, but she had to sleep. She was haunted by the memory of awakening one night with one leg hanging off the bed where the monsters could grab it. Fear alone made her hearing more acute. She could hear breathing before the intruder broke in. Her skin felt the slightest temperature change as the cool night air penetrated her space, a sign that the window was being pried open. She refused to concentrate on anything else knowing her very survival hung by the thread of her willpower.

As fatigue flowed in, she fought back. Singing soundless songs worked at first, making sure each word was correct or she started over. The words were too familiar to prevent sleep for long. Lists of what her brothers had done to make her angry required more attention and were good for an additional thirty minutes. The time they locked her in the closet when her parents were out could sustain her for fifteen minutes more. Her body ached for rest. It was so hard to resist. She didn't go easily as each ounce of determination was exhausted, until finally resistance was futile. Still she fought as her lids descended. The images faded as she finally succumbed, once again, and slept. The battle well fought she could rest, knowing she gave her all.

Until tomorrow, that is.

CANDY STORES AND ME

Some would define the essence of Brooklyn as the Dodgers or the social escalator that is the public education system. But for me it was the corner candy store. My father's father worked in one for a time before he assumed the American dream and had his own house painting company. My wife's grandparents survived the depression by working the 6am to 11 pm schedule of the candy store and living in the small apartment above. Everyone needed their cigarettes and newspaper, even when the job market plunged in parallel with the stock market. In the tag team world of family ownership, one was always in the store, while the other tended to the kids and dinner upstairs.

In its simplest form the candy store was the most unhealthy of enterprises, living predominantly on the sale of sugar and tobacco.

But what sugar!

Candies of every shape, color, texture, even sugared and dyed water filling little wax bottles, requiring the gleeful biting off of the bottle neck to suck out the succulent sweetness. There were multicolored buttons of pure sugar somehow pasted to long rolls of what looked like adding machine paper. Long thin plastic tubes held tiny sugar balls suitable for eating or shooting at friends. This was the ultimate impulse buy, as rows upon rows of candy were the first things to greet you on entering and the last when leaving the store.

Behind the counter were the stacks of beige ice cream cones, the slightly darker and so much more delicious sugar cones, and the broad walk-away cones.

Bet you've never heard of a walk- away. For those with deprived childhoods, defined as not growing up in Brooklyn, a walk-away was to my memory a tube of any flavor ice cream scooped by a shiny metal cylinder which with a squeeze of the handle delivered the ice cream to its special cone, leaving a central depression that extended half way down. Nature abhors a vacuum and so does the ice cream counter, as the empty space was filled with syrup—highly concentrated, viscous, compressed sugar molecules—and topped with whipped cream and a cherry. In my memory, this cost the outrageous price of 35 cents, but was worth every cavity producing slurp.

Higher on the economic ladder were chocolate malteds, thick and foamy and having the fig-leaf of nutrition, milk. They were served along with the metal container in which they were mixed, guaranteeing a refill. The best of all was the next step up. As if all the goodness of a malted could not be surpassed, add a large scoop of chocolate ice cream to the glass and line the top with whipped cream before pouring in the thick, foamy chocolate ambrosia from the bottomless metal container, and you had a float. In my household this was reserved for birthdays or bar mitzvah celebrations.

And it was worth the wait!

In the back of the store was the soda case filled with small and quart sized bottles of everything except the word *diet*. After a summer's day of endless ball games, we would regroup in the candy store for a soda. I recall some of the bigger kids downing a quart bottle of Hire's root beer in one sitting. Perhaps that's where the quintessential pre-teen habit of "burp-talking" originated.

Candy stores evolved from selling the big three: cigarettes, sugar and newspapers, to include food, adopting the modest diminutive *luncheonette*. This meant that there was always chicken or tuna salad, fresh rye bread and half sour pickles in the refrigerator behind the counter. Seating was expanded from the seven or eight red topped, high counter stools. Perhaps they seemed high because as a kid I wasn't. The metal step was needed to hoist my too-candy-rounded body up onto the seat, which was soft enough to be comfortable and impervious enough to be clean.

My first encounter with the restaurant aspect came at Sones', the candy store one block from PS 180 and owned by a classmate's father. Most candy stores showed pride of ownership by being named for their owners and not their locations, usually in my recollection the first names like the euphonious Lou's Luncheonette. The joke at the time, revealing more of our economic status than the operation of Sones', was that a coke there was 5 cents, with glass a quarter—followed by howling laughter at the outrageous and unattainable price of 25 cents.

We usually walked home from school alone in the small town mindset of early 1950s. One day when I was in the early grades, my mother was waiting for me with a large umbrella. It was one of those late fall stormy days with horizontal rain that would penetrate our yellow slickers with their metal eye and hook closures, our high blue boots and even our rain hats. She shepherded my older brother, my sister and me under the umbrella, but instead of walking home she guided us through the crowd around Sones' candy story into the back where she had somehow reserved a table. There on the shiny Formica we ate huge, deliciously different tuna salad sandwiches. I don't know how tuna can be so exciting. Perhaps it was the additives: was it celery? Or pieces of relish? Or something other than our usual Hellman's mayonnaise? Or that the tuna was chopped to almost a paste? It was exotic and wonderful both for the taste and the surprise of it all.

Candy stores provided the first jobs for many a high school student, and I was no exception. Bernie's luncheonette was my first steady job. Carrying shellac cans for my father didn't count because that work was expected and not compensated. On the corner of 48th street and 16th avenue, Bernie's was just down the block from our new rental apartment. I could easily be there every day after school to refill the sugar and napkin dispensers, fill the soda case by lugging cases of quart bottles from the basement and wet mopping the entire store.

The real work took place on Sunday mornings. I was there at 5-30 am with a metal hook attached to a wooden handle, pulling bales of newspapers wrapped tightly in wires to the wooden stand, just after the papers had been thrown from delivery trucks. Inside the still closed-for-business store I would snip the wire, line up the myriad sections of the New York Times, and Daily News, assemble them into completed papers, and stack as many as I could fit on the wooden newspaper stand outside the front door. The rest were stacked inside, ready to refill the stand when the morning rush began.

Strangely there was no concern for theft in this neighborhood store where the majority of patrons were on a first name basis with the gregarious Bernie. In my memory, I was paid for the week's work after all the papers were set up with Bernie handing me a bank envelope, the kind that has a top flap, filled with the colossal sum of $13, paid as six two dollar bills and one single. (This was a time when I could and did buy three shirts for $4 each at a Wallach's fire sale. It took a good washing to cleanse the smoky fragrance but the sense of pride they represented remained, knowing they were the product of my labor and that pay envelope.) The whipped cream on this 'malted' was that Bernie would make me any fountain drink I wanted after work. These were the teen years when the biggest weight problem was how to gain some, and Bernie did his best to help.

Small towns had their general stores or pharmacies with a soda fountain, but the candy store seemed unique to Brooklyn. I knew no one who grew up in my time who didn't have a story or immutable memory of the candy store, part of our youth, part of our growing up, an inseparable part of Brooklyn.

MY BAR MITZVAH

Memories of my Bar Mitzvah are seen in the rear view mirror, fogged by fifty-seven years. There is no family lore to bolster my recollection since it was unremarkable as life-cycle events go. As with many remote occasions recalled in snapshots and not streaming video, the gaps must be filled with supposition.

We lived a lower middle class existence in a rented first floor apartment in Boro Park, a misspelled Brooklyn neighborhood of private homes. My Bar Mitzvah celebration took place in the front room of that apartment. But I am getting ahead of myself.

I studied with Rabbi Goldberg in one room of his rented apartment several blocks away. I remember kicking a chunk of ice most of the way home one day until it was too small to separate from the ice and slush on Fourteenth Avenue. I remember the Rabbi's study as brown and overly warm. I remember him chewing apples while his false teeth separated from his jaw. I remember him saying: "Grass will grow on my palm before Gustman graduates from this school," referring to the Hebrew lessons that preceded Bar Mitzvah preparation. I remember skipping classes when the weather was good and football games were plentiful. Despite my poor attendance record and whatever grew inside his gloves, I did graduate prepared sufficiently to recite my week's Torah portion.

We approached my grandfather's Orthodox Schul, a converted storefront filled with benches and a lectern. Most seats were filled as my family came in; but I recall my grandfather, a small gray haired man with an even grayer moustache, guiding me to the front row and helping me on with my tallis. I don't specifically recall a separation of men and women though I'm fairly sure the orthodox custom was observed. In my memory, the prayer books had no vowels and were unreadable to me. The men "davened" quickly and soon I was ushered to the lectern. My only recollection is that of wearing a grayish suit and if not wowing the crowd with my performance, not screwing up enough to be an embarrassment to my grandfather or myself.

We adjourned—after schnapps, sponge cake and herring were served—to my house. The front room where my sister slept had been transformed into a bright party room for all the neighborhood kids, with a u-shaped table open to the hallway from which all manner of kid-food emerged. Hot dogs in blankets and knishes were definitely represented because I recall asking my very happy mother for more and her smile disappeared as she said that was all we had.

The kids then adjourned to a nearby candy store where, armed with a twenty dollar bill held in a death grip, I bought floats and malteds and ice cream Sundays for all the guests. Now *that* was a party.

AN IMAGINED DREAM

At fourteen I was in high school, liked athletics, the New York Giants and was on the cusp of dating. Saturday was movie day and groups of boys and girls would go to the Loewe's Theater on New Utrecht Avenue in Brooklyn. We alternated between the girls choosing, usually some Rock Hudson, Doris Day romance and the boys' choice of the macho horror movie of the week.

All was well until one night; I went to sleep and was awakened by splashing. Since the bathtub was the only source of deep water, I walked into the bathroom and there he was—seven feet high with green scales, a long tail and horizontal slits for eyes, the Creature from the Black Lagoon, whose movie we had seen that weekend.

"Hey," I said. "I left you in the movies hours ago. What are you doing in my bathtub?"

"I should be in your kitchen sink?" it said sounding like a combination of Woody Allen and Jackie Mason.

"But you're getting water on my mother's floor; she works hard to keep it clean."

"And your nose is running, but do I complain?" said the intruder.

"You have no right to wake me up and mess up my house," I said.

"You should see the crap you left on the movie theater floor. I slipped on the melted bon-bons and nearly broke my neck," it said.

"OK, I won't see any more really scary movies if you promise to stay out of my dreams," I said.

"Your dreams scare the hell out of me too. I'm going back to the swamp," it said, and never returned.

THE BUSINESS AT HAND

As I sit on my bed struggling to extract the secrets of Quantitative Analysis from the textbook indenting my lap, my mother comes in with a worried look on her face: "We need you to run Dad's business until the doctor says he's recovered from his heart attack. Just pick up the shellac and deliver it to his customers between classes." Then more slowly," We're barely squeaking by as is. If we shut down even for a few weeks our customers will disappear. I'm sorry but I don't know what else to do." She hugs me and begins to cry.

I am a senior at Brooklyn College, a commuter school, and have been accepted to medical school class of 1969 pending my fall semester grades. For some reason, which cannot now be recalled, I have taken Quantitative Analysis, a course that demands more lab time and precision than I can conjure. If I don't improve the pending C or slip further, I may as well choose shellac sales as my life's work.

I guess the deliveries could be done if I'm out of the house by 7a.m. and back in time for 10a.m. classes. Afternoons are out because I have so many labs. I say with little conviction," I'll take care of it."

My mother is the front office. She takes the orders and calls them in to Ben Gart. He makes the shellac in a small, dark, East New York factory filled with the sounds of rubber belts, which reach out from loud motors like tentacles, spinning the mixing blades that stir 500 gallon wooden vats filled with shellac. The factory air is both dusty and intoxicating being saturated with pulverized bug parts and alcohol, the essence of shellac. Ben was my employer during almost every school vacation since junior high school. I was the lowest level employee, carrying 50 pound bags of bone dry and loading cans and cartons of shellac-filled jars into trucks. Now I will be returning as a paying customer, the one to be helped and not the helper.

The next morning the alarm jolts me awake at 6 a.m. I arrive at the shellac factory to some loud kidding. "You've lost a lot of weight, Sam (my father's name)," said Willie, a fifty something black man who has worked there as long as I can remember. He is known for regaling everyone with stories of intricate sexual gymnastics. After one particularly communicative morning, I realized that I may never look at a rocking chair the same way again. Ben Gart, the owner, is in his early forties. He is an athlete and loves to talk about his weekend baseball games. He is as usual dressed in overalls covered with the unavoidable layer of grit that also covers every inch of the factory, except the closed off business office. He smiles broadly and says, "So how's the business man?" He laughs then gets down to brass tacks. "I'll give you this load, but you'll have to pay cash for the next. Your dad wasn't exactly current on his bills."

The shellac cans line the hallway. I ask Willie if he can load up the car trunk. He mumbles something, including the word "uppity," and walks away. There are snickers from the other employees.

I drive about thirty minutes to a small store, 'Lieberman and Son, Painters'. Since his father retired, the son in his late forties runs the business. He greets me pleasantly. He has known me since I was four or five, old enough to accompany my father on deliveries. He is tall and has the broad shoulders of a painter. He lifts the five gallon shellac containers with much less effort than I employ. We unload together as he inquires about my father's health. "Tell him I want to see him back here soon, so you can go back to studying. If I did more of that, I wouldn't have to do mule work for a living." He pays the $192 bill mostly in twenties. I look up and down the street before getting into my car, certain there are armed robbers everywhere.

I make a point of going back to the factory, even if it will make me late for my first class. I walk in and tell Ben Gart that I am here to pay for the shellac. I hand him $100, the full amount owed for this morning's product. His face is a mask of surprise, most of it genuine. I return home with $92 profit and hand it to my mother. Her shocked expression is testimony to how rarely this has occurred in the past. Unlike my father, there has been no trip to the racetrack, or Ebinger's bakery, or the grocery store to buy an otherwise unaffordable standing rib roast. And there are no calls home from Ben Gart suggesting that if the bills aren't paid there will be no more credit extended.

My mother is saving the money I bring home as if it is the last she will see for a while, which is not far from the truth. We eat lamb stew every night, the cheapest meat.

The studies have been a challenge. Our final exam consists of determining the weight to several decimal points of an "unknown," a vial of blue powder and granules. I am horrified to notice a faint blue tint to the sleeve of my lab coat. My lab measurements are shown to be quantitatively lacking and I get the first D of my college career.

This is followed one week later by a letter from Dean Hench of the Medical College of Virginia, Admissions Department.

Dear Mr. Gustman,
I was quite disappointed to see your current grade in Quantitative Analysis. Is there a reason why we should not reconsider your early acceptance...?" Have I blown it? Is my whole career derailed before the first hour of anatomy? In desperation I sit at the kitchen table and with a trembling hand, write a response.

"Dear Dean Hench,
This is not to explain away the D I got in Quantitative Analysis, but to put it in perspective...."

A few days later I get the Dean's response apologizing for the first letter and wishing me well in coping with my home situation. I am still accepted, the D notwithstanding.

My father is allowed to resume lifting after three months. I go back to being a college senior and a vacation-time, low-level employee of the shellac factory. Willie even forgives me for "puttin' on an attitude" and tells me about new uses for goose grease that I couldn't quite understand. Nothing changes in my father's work habits, and the $400 that my mother managed to squirrel away is soon needed to pay for more shellac. When I leave for medical school, my father applies for a hack license so he can drive a cab whenever his supply of shellac is denied.

I am never again asked to run his business, which survives for three years, the remainder of his life.

I earn money in med school by performing quantitative assessments of blood specimens in the ER lab.

CONEY ISLAND

My memories of Coney Island are gauzy and sweet like the cotton candy available on the board walk. Most trips occurred in the summer when fireworks made each Tuesday night into the 4th of July. The amusements evoke magical words like Steeplechase which had gathered all manner of rides and thrills under one roof. It contained "the horses" a near death thrill ride of mechanical horses racing on the very edge of the rooftops, riders held in place by a lap belt of insufficient tightness or strength. There was the unspeakably terrifying cyclone with impossible drops made on an ancient wooden structure to which we grudgingly entrusted our lives. The parachute jump completed the circuit of "eat later" thrills—if you didn't want to encounter your lunch again.

As a teenager, my friends and I would go by subway to Stillwell Avenue, the heart of Coney Island where facilities like Washington Baths were inexpensive and provided the equivalent of day camp without counselors. Squash, handball, two pools, steam baths, and the beach provided all that a kid could ask. Only in later years did I realize that the cough that followed visits to the Coney Island beach was probably related to the pollution coming from Norton's Point, the trash dump just upstream.

By far the best part of Coney Island was the food, spelled Nathan's. Now a household word through the miracle of franchising, it was then unique. People came from surrounding boroughs to sample the original Nathan's hot dogs. There were always 50 or more sizzling at any given moment in several long rows on their huge grill, the smell serving as an advertisement and an appetizer to those waiting in line. To this day I savor the first bite through the casing that pops just a little as you release all the wonderful juices inside. The French fries — replete with a small red triton to spear them— were cooked in oil that was reputed to contain honey, the secret ingredient that made them so irresistible. Everything was piping hot, which was especially appreciated on winter days.

For the more adventurous there were the hamburgers or roast beef sandwiches, of which my friend Robbie is said to have downed twelve at one sitting winning a bet and a world class case of indigestion. The delicacy par excellence, the lobster roll with its 75 cent price, was for the wealthy or those who just couldn't resist it. There was always the Schatzkin's knishes store right next door, providing an extension of the ethnic smorgasbord that was Nathan's.

Everyone I know has a Coney Island story. My own occurred when I was in college and a friend and I were trying to learn an entire semester of organic chemistry in one Christmas vacation by staying up all night studying and sleeping during the day. Benzene rings danced in our heads and eventually we could stand no more. It was 3 a.m. and there was a snow storm raging outside. After a week of abnegation this seemed the perfect time to go to Nathan's. The slow drive through empty, snow lined streets was uneventful. Even parking was not a problem; yet we had to stand in line behind groups of equally frozen customers, each of whom couldn't make it through the night without a Nathan's hot dog.

Only in Coney Island.

DRIVE

It was a favor bestowed grudgingly when my brother, one year older, agreed to drive me anywhere. Late one night after my eighteenth birthday, a newly laminated driver's license in my pocket, I found myself once again in the passenger seat. We had just dropped off a friend of mine and a surly silence pressurized the car. Without warning he pulled to the side and I braced for a verbal assault, when he said, "You drive." I got out and walked to the driver's door still uncertain if this was a prank and he would pull away, but he had already slid over to my usual seat.

I slipped behind the gray smooth steering wheel of the ten year old 1952 Ford, onto the L-shaped plastic folding seat that rested on torn plaid upholstery. I adjusted nothing, trying to be as unobtrusive as possible.

No seat belt restrained my movements as I pushed in the clutch and bounced into first gear. The avenue was deserted at 1 AM as I twisted to my left to double check for oncoming traffic. "Use your mirrors," he said. This was a challenge since the right side mirror had long ago been sacrificed to a passing Brooklyn truck.

We drove for almost an hour, he not wanting to sleep and the driver in a parallel world of magic carpets and freedom.

"Turn here."

"Left at the corner. A little wider."

"Trucks have air brakes so give them room," he said.

Wide awake, I could have gone on and on when he said, "Pull over here. I'll drive home." Unsaid was that Dad did not know or specifically approve of me driving the family car, the business car—often so loaded with shellac cans that the rear barely cleared the ground— the only car.

So this was a surprise, a treat, a misdemeanor, a bond.

"Thanks," I said, really meaning it.

"Move your ass over," he replied.

DRIVE ON

Two years later the competition for the family car was no more. My brother had decided to invest fifty dollars of the summer money, which he earned bussing tables, in a deeply used Buick. It was the third such car, each poised at the front gate of the junk yard. He would squeeze the last few months from these nearly moribund specimens, then sell each for a few dollars and buy its twin. The common marker was a black stream of exhaust, like its own personal tornado, that announced his approach from blocks away.

I was in my senior year at Brooklyn College applying to six medical schools, when Hahnemann invited me to Philadelphia for an interview. My brother—anxious for any excuse to be away from our father—volunteered to drive me. We left with hours to spare and it was a good thing. A trail of smoke marked our departure from Brooklyn. He knew the cause of the black contrail was oil leaking into the engine cylinders and burning up. This both fouled the air and eventually deprived the engine of lubrication causing it to overheat.

"I'll drive and you watch the oil gauge," he said. As we cruised over the Verrazano Bridge and eventually onto the New Jersey Turnpike all seemed clear sailing—if you looked ahead! Behind was a dystopic view of the world obscured by a black haze dense enough for other cars to put on their wipers and yell words that were drowned out by the grinding Buick valves. A few miles later, I noticed the oil pressure dropping and the engine temperature rising in unison. We pulled to the side of the road as I began to fear missing my first and possibly only medical school interview. My brother strode to the trunk, which opened with noisy protest, and took out a five gallon metal can filled with oil and a long necked aluminum funnel. We opened the hood and rapidly refilled the oil until the dip stick was no longer dry. Then we slowed the flow but put in enough so the oil just overflowed as the dip stick was replaced. We were back in the car, with a distinct petroleum scent, in less than ten minutes.

Three more oil stops later we were at the doors of Hahnemann, an ancient set of red brick buildings in an unfashionable section of Philadelphia. We went in, washed off the oil residue in the nearby rest room and were offered a tour of the medical school before the interview. My brother agreed to join. Past the lobby was a hallway that led to the anatomy lab. The double doors were pulled open to reveal rows of aluminum tables covered with brown rubber sheets. From beneath each, extended feet with a tag attached to the great toe. I glimpsed my brother's ivory, sweating face as he did a perfect 180 degree turn that would have made a Marine proud. He lurched back through the door and spent the entire time reading magazines in the waiting room.

The interview was neither a great success nor a disaster and we drove back, both glad to be leaving. The drive home was remarkable only for one half-hour Turnpike stop to cool down the engine, which attracted a New Jersey State Trooper. He was eventually satisfied that we were not vagrants and sent us off with a lecture on the value of engine maintenance. Within the month, the Buick polluted no more and was replaced by a fifty dollar Chevy that could have been its twin.

YARN

She sits knitting
A shapeless piece that grows
As the skein unravels,
As she unravels.

In younger years knitting was done
When her eager hands were free.
She could knit and visit, or while sponge cake baked,
Filling the house with goodness and purpose.

Knitting set the rhythm of the house, of the family.
So automatic, so natural, it belonged,
Woven into the fabric of the home and all who called it
home.
It set the pace and tone, marking time, stitch by stitch.

How could a conversation be rushed?
How could an interaction be abrupt
When the metronome that was the knitting needles
Created a slower, intimate cadence?

Learning as a pre-teen, a rite of passage,
Her skill, gleaned from generations past,
From her grandmother, who learned from hers.
She had honed her skill in the days since.

Through the years each event was celebrated
By a sweater, with square wooden buttons
Or slippers that separated skin
From the frozen tiles below.

Or an Afghan, the colors of the summer sky,
Or the green of a garden in early spring.
No baby entered her world
Without a blanket of pastel softness.

As the yarn unraveled so did the commotion
And purpose of a growing houseful.
For purpose had a destination,
Which claimed those formerly here.

Each house of the now dispersed brood
Warmed with the fruits of her labor, her love.
But they were scattered, their worlds
Expanding as hers contracted.

The family if not unraveled had been stretched
Afar, so the garment so carefully crafted,
So well fitting, was now shapeless,
Strings pulled hither and yon.

The careful weave, the web so tight
Slowly becoming undone as the clock ticked.
As the yarn unraveled, slowly, inexorably,
So did her ability to recall.

Shedding the new, but still anchored
By the knots of events long past,
The act and comfort of knitting
Residing deep within, she continued.

She traveled a familiar path
To an ill-remembered station;
Being satisfied by the routine
She weaved from wool long possessed.

The ball grew smaller
As did her ability to see it clearly,
Or hear the phone, or sense temperature
With her "asbestos" fingers.

Yet she labored on,
Making it mattered not what,
Unraveling the yarn of her life,
To the cadence of the needles.

LOVE

WAITING FOR THE BUS-PART 1

Late fall turns to winter, as we wait in the cold for a glimpse of the bus we cannot board. We stand in front of the Medical Education Building, two first-year students struggling on a journey to the semester's end, ever receding into the distance. Along with the endless tasks, we endure the isolation of the study carrel and the dorm room shared only at sleeping time—isolated from those we love, from those who give comfort, from home.

My roommate and I, both accepted from Brooklyn College to The Medical College of Virginia, have pictures of girls—soon to be wives—smiling encouragement on our desks. The pictures also speak to our innermost longings, foretelling a better life to come, one that banishes loneliness. Is it any wonder that most relationships progress after entering the cauldron that is medical school?

We know, feel, ache for the balm that is a Trailways bus ride away. Weighed down with heavy tomes and with a vague scent of formaldehyde, which permeates our clothing and hair, we wait. It is a sanity break from the endless studying, labs, cadavers. Even prisoners get to exercise in the yard. Ours is a day-dreaming interval made more real by the magic carpet, the Trailways bus. We know its path and schedule. We strain to see it as the time draws near; squinting to be sure it is our bus, that it says *New York* in orange and white letters above the front window.

Confirmation of sighting is needed by both to be credible. We verify, then watch it with a blend of hope and melancholy that lingers long after its shape fades in the distance. We cannot board, not yet. We can only envision the banquet, but not taste a morsel; for we have endless things to do, to prove to others that we have learned. Our self-imposed sentence of hard labor is only partially served.

But we know with an unshakable certainty that our bus will come. We will board and be carried to the place we yearn to be. This certainty, reinforced by the proximity of our Trailways chariot, gives strength to persevere and plan a future where all that matters most is not a bus ride away.

WAITING FOR THE BUS-PART 2.

It is now June and the first dose of medicine has been absorbed. I have survived and will be invited back for more. Board exams have been taken, nothing to be done except await the grades, creating a vacuum in time. It is a Friday night and I arrive at my cousin's house and store textbooks, my one suitcase poised. I am to sleep at this house tonight and take the first Trailways bus to New York, my bus, in the morning.

Much has changed. A reunion and a wedding wait. I sit through dinner barely aware of what is entering my mouth; then as my mind races, I pace. Finally I blurt out that I can't wait until morning. Against all advice I call and find that a midnight bus has seats and we have plenty of time to get there. "It may not be safe; you won't sleep; why not wait and go at a sensible time tomorrow," they plead, but their words bounce like pebbles off a tank. I need to go; I can go; I damn sure will go. With great reluctance they drive me to the bus station and make sure I get on safely. There are so few passengers that I have both first row seats. The seat, designed for the compact structure of those of a distant age, does not allow the legs of a six foot two man to fit. I drape them over the barrier in front, feeling like a prize buck being tied to the front of the pickup truck. Sleep is intermittent at best, interrupted by the inevitable numbness of my limbs and neck stiffness that follows my contortion.

By 6 a.m. we approach the brown funnel of air that sits atop New York City like an inverted ice cream cone. I will feeling back into abused parts and head for the subway, for home. With my suitcase between my knees I stand out from the early morning commuters and thus am doubly alert should I attract unwanted attention. Everything I own in the world resides in a suitcase three feet in length. I realize that if that suitcase is lost there will be little physical record that I ever existed.

I drink in the city from below: the sounds, the people, the smells so deliciously familiar. All thought of sleep gone. I enter my parent's apartment with a key and hear my mother say "Alan, did you forget something?" my brother having just left. She has her glasses in her hand and looks with puzzlement at my grinning face. When she puts them on she shouts, "Paul!!!   Sam, Paul is home! When? How? It's so early. Let me get you something to eat..." I know in that instant how right it was to take the midnight bus; how good it is to be home; how this could not, should not have waited until a more sensible time. Neither would my marriage. Everything I wished for is here at the other end of my Trailways bus.

THE FIVE SENSES—WRITING COURSE ASSIGNMENT

Describe a person you have loved using the five senses.

So what do you have in mind today, Paul? As you know, we at the Auto-mate store can create your dreams and place them in any body you desire.

I'll go retro, I said.

I want to see sweetness radiate, a smile before she smiles.

I want the sound of listening, concern.

I want the savory smell of welcome to dinner for all who wish to cross our threshold.

I want a touch that says you and you alone.

I want the good taste of satisfaction when we share.

And he made....Marilyn.

THE PROPOSAL

Medical school is a lonely slog, days jammed full of tasks, nights never long enough to learn everything. The first year was especially stressful for me, being away from home for the first time and from Marilyn, whose smiling picture warmed my desk and reminded me what I was missing. We met waiting for a grilled cheese sandwich in the Brooklyn College cafeteria. I first saw her radiant smile when I told her she was a gentleman for offering to let me go first. Perhaps I was so skinny she thought I wouldn't make it to the cashier if I didn't get some nourishment soon. After being invited by her friend to a fix-up party, M and I were together for the rest of my senior year.

The isolation of the unmarried medical students resulted in a hastening of the heart, so that those dating became pinned, pinning begat engagements and those resulted in accelerated wedding dates.

The road blocks in our relationship were more parental than practical. The common wisdom of the time was that girls in general and marriage in particular distracted from the mental monasticism necessary to graduate medical school. Taking a wife in the first two years of school—in the parental view—was if not committing professional suicide, then severely hobbling your chance of success. Parents could emphasize this caveat in ways, from verbal disapproval to refusing to pay for or attend a wedding; that is how serious some were about the dangers of entering the marriage morass.

For me, having a negative net worth and no cash reserves, marriage seemed an impossibility. I earned a few dollars working evenings at the front desk of the Medical Education Building where duties were so few I could study most of the time. Loneliness grew as the year went on despite a visit from Marilyn, who flew in for a day, and a wonderful two week Christmas vacation that emphasized what I was missing. By April I found myself lingering on the steps of the Medical Education Building looking at Trailways buses and trying to see if they were bound for New York. If so, I watched as they drove into the horizon and I could make them out no longer.

Collect phone calls to Marilyn—since her parents had allowed her a generous "Paul phone allowance"—were my only source of sustenance. I would never want to hang up and would talk about almost anything so I could hear her voice a few minutes longer.

I spoke with my brother and sister from time to time. One call in April had both of them on the line. I was moaning about how lonely it was and how I would have to wait until the end of my second year to get married. "Are you sure you love Marilyn and want to get married?" asked my brother. "Very sure," I replied. "So what are you waiting for?" said my sister and brother. "Well.... "I had no real answer. Marilyn had graduated and was teaching, so we would have some income. We had lots of married med students, some with kids, who were doing fine. The ones who dropped out were usually incredibly lonely or decided they were in med. school for the wrong reasons: "Dad was a doctor and it was assumed........" I didn't know a single person who dropped out because of the stresses caused by marriage.

That was the moment my life changed. All obstacles became fading mist in the morning sun as I called Marilyn, told of the marriage proposal—made first by my sibs—and would she marry me. She answered yes to the whole family's proposal. With the speed of one who has thought about the issue previously, my delighted mother-in-law-to-be minimized the difficulties of organizing a wedding in four months.

The problem was my parents. I called, strengthened by love and desperation. My father answered. "I'm getting married," I blurted out, which was followed by a painful, palpable silence. Finally he said to my mother but intentionally audible on my end of the phone, "He says he getting married. He doesn't ask, just says he getting married." He then repeats this to me. My mother takes the phone and a disloyal delight comes through as she extracts what few details exist.

So I've just turned 21, have skipped the whole engagement delay and have survived telling my parents the news. When I come home for the summer vacation, I hear my father on the phone with an uncle,"So he called me like a man and said, 'I'm getting married.'"

It took a committee to get me to make the move. Having Marilyn pay the five dollars for the wedding license is a story for another day.

SOFT

Soft as the barely touching lips
In the gentlest of kiss
When passion is spent
But a new step awaits.

Bonding of souls
Expressing more. Wanting
To share the joy surging
From a place awakened.

Soft as the words "I do,"
Gentle as a breeze
After a spring rain
Shared with all who came.

In a near dream
As weight and warmth
Of the oath descend
Two lives, now one.

Soft as the touch
Of a mother, spent
In the birthing
Of her first child

Oh so gently counting
The fingers and toes
Meeting anew the one
She has known so long.

Soft is their prayer
To the blessed one
Who allowed them all
To reach this day.

Soft as the blankets swathing
New life, bathed in the rain
Of joyous tears, to welcome
A grandchild, grand indeed!

Soft as the breath of life
That changes theirs forever
Graduates all, to a new level
Of duty, of stature, of love.

OLD BOSSY

She wasn't the most beautiful or modern and she'd been around the block. She protruded in all the right places for an old girl, still classy in that last decade way. This was her second time around…. for her odometer that is. The shiny black '59 Chevy Biscayne had logged more than one hundred thousand miles when she came South as part of our wedding package.

She had been tuned like a Stradivarius by my father-in-law who changed the oil every three thousand miles, before it was in fashion. We took ownership and responsibility for this grand dame in 1966 when she ferried two ridiculously young newlyweds three hundred sixty miles from New York to the Jarrett Apartments, medical student housing in Richmond Virginia.

A few of our fellow students parked late model sports cars or sedans at Jarrett, but there were enough aged autos that we felt right at home. While I car pooled the twenty minutes to the Medical Education Building, Marilyn made the drive all across the county to teach science to Junior High School students. As one of the few Jewish teachers in Henrico county— yes they did ask— she was assigned to the one school that had a Jewish principal. Marilyn liked the school and students but didn't enjoy the long drive in heavy traffic.

She enjoyed it less when Bossy's old carburetor acted up and the car refused to start. Taught by an expert mechanic, her father, Marilyn would open the hood, unscrew the wing nut and take out the air filter. Then she would use a wooden clothes pin to keep the butterfly valve open. This would usually do it and the low throaty vibrations of the engine 'catching' would replace the recurrent bronchial cough.

With time the sputtering starts became more frequent, sometimes requiring a tow home. The third time that Marilyn's came home in the cab of an AAA rescue vehicle, we knew that Bossy's days were numbered. We shopped at Dominion Chevrolet, a West Richmond dealership where the cars smelled of newness and purred at startup. Our new Nova was a deep blue color. It fit our budget. You see, my in-laws had allowed us the same amount for our wedding as they spent on their first daughter's, four years prior. We thought it best to spend half on the wedding and save the other $2,500 for a car, when and if it was needed. It was, and sooner than we had imagined.

Bossy became the backup. In protest and depression she began to weep coolant from the radiator, which when dry would give off a high pitched whistle and steam would pour from the engine. Also, she would throw a tantrum and have an endless coughing fit when we turned her off. The mechanic said this was "dieseling," but sounded more like retching, as black smoke emerged from the tail pipe and the whole car rocked side to side for a minute or more, making a protest sound of *chunka-flop, chunka-flop.*

With regret we decided that the time had arrived for Bossy to go. We spruced her up for her date with the used car buyer. We filled her radiator with coolant and left the engine running as we awaited his arrival. A chunky man, cigar clenched in one corner of his mouth, he opened the hood, looked around briefly, then inside and said "Twenty-fahv dollas."

"What!" we cried in unison. We then began to list her good features: "she's got a great body, is quick on the pick-up and is quite musical with a fully functioning radio. She's worth at least a hundred fifty." We were desperate to close the deal before the true state of affairs was revealed. "Twenty-fahv dollas," he said.

Just then, time ran out. The radiator went dry and a loud whistle—not unlike the one that signals the end of a work shift—emerged from beneath the hood. We rushed to shut off the car as steam began to pour from the radiator. Bossy shook side to side in loud protest: *chunka-flop, chunka-flop*. The sidewalk detail was lost in the black exhaust cloud.

Red-faced, we looked up at the buyer who said, "Twenty-fahv dollas."

YES

Tasks arise in the course of life, many are burdensome and for the sole benefit of others. For these my wife always volunteers. Her hand goes up before the asking has reached its first comma. "We need someone to make lunch for a group of homeless girls"—her hand is up—*comma*—"because ..." "We are having a shower for"—her hand is up, suggesting areas that need volunteers, the first one, of course, being herself.

Craft workshops are offered to friends, office co-workers, kids without homes. They become times of bonding and result in creations that amaze the new artists with discovered skills and new-found pride. *Organize* is the operative word, often applied to family vacations, surprise events and even talent shows (second prize went to Jeremy age 12 for burping the alphabet).

The dining room table is lined with Algebra for Dummies, Intermediate Algebra—I guess for the slightly more enlightened—and geometry textbooks. Marilyn found out that a lovely breakfast waitress who has served up eggs and smiles for years was trying to go back to school and become a nurse. Standing in her way was a brick wall made of binomial equations and cosines. " I can tutor you, "came from Marilyn just as she was automatically beginning to raise her hand in the restaurant, a problematic gesture since the waitress had not yet discussed this plan with her employers. The first two-hour tutorial went on for five. Marilyn was up in the middle of the night trying to remember how to derive cosines of each angle of a right triangle.

Centerpieces are her specialty. Rarely has there been an event not already pre-themed and pre-ordered, for which she has not made all or part of the centerpieces. Perhaps it's the unused creative energy built up from years of not having her gift shop, *For Give and For Get*. Today there are fifteen cinnamon brooms in my entryway for an unspecified future workshop.

Yes to charities, yes to the needy, yes to friends and relatives and relatives of friends. But the best of all was forty-nine years ago, when she signed on for a long journey of unknown destination and answered yes when I asked her to marry me. She even said yes when asked for the five bucks to pay for the license.

AN ADVENTURE

Driving for my wife is a continual adventure with an uncertain ending. She has driven all her adult life and loves the freedom of movement, the control. She loves being able to alter the route to fit in one more stop. The destination is never a foregone conclusion, however. Where it ends is often not where intended, or when.

We are all born with certain intellectual gifts, which my brother refers to as chips in our personal computers. My wife has recall of every restaurant meal eaten, where, how prepared, and certainty of whether she would order it again. She can recall every holiday gift given, with size and color decisions, and why they were made. She has a unique understanding of people and with rare exception responds to situations with sensivity and compassion that are intuitively astute. Her computer is so packed with the well functioning chips—that make her such a wonderful person, friend and wife—there is no room for the GPS. She is one of those rare individuals who are directionally impaired to the extent that they are predictably wrong. Left and right are interchangeable terms resulting in random turns of the car. North, south, east and west are concepts absorbed after great thought, analysis of the sun's position, and map study; with resolution arriving long after the decision point is past.

She has known about this for years but has begun to accept it only recently. I recall a carpooling teacher forty years ago saying, "Well, Marilyn, ready to try it again?" Our daughter has resorted to pointing when providing directions. Her Mom's reaction was, "Just tell me which way to go," to which my daughter dutifully replied, "Turn left at the next corner." After the car went to the right, the hand signals resumed. Through the years my wife has regaled us with stories of new places discovered while aiming elsewhere, usually delivered with a laugh or sardonic frown. Some parts of town, best unvisited, have been explored before being, thankfully, exited safely. I have discouraged her request for the vanity license plate *IMLOST*. Only occasionally is frustration expressed, when the mark is missed by so wide a margin as to create a useless foray. She shares an optimism and energy inherited from her father, a man who drove for two hours to get a part, at the end of an exhausting day of repairing something or other for his children. Her quarry is usually in the realm of craft project supplies or the perfect gift, each journey beginning with high hopes and vague directions.

I am much better behaved in the car when I drive. There is no slamming my foot on the imaginary passenger-side brake or diving for cover when I am actually in control of the vehicle; so my wife by default becomes the navigator. In days of yore when an AAA *triptik* was necessary for a long journey, she would have the map unfurled, rotating it so our direction was always up, obviating the need to deal with those pesky concepts of north, south, east and west. These days the I-Pad, with its most helpful flashing blue dot, provides both accurate directions and space in the front seat formerly occupied by *triptiks*. The modern technology would seem to solve all issues when she is in the car alone if she:

a. remembered to take the I-Pad.
b. knew the exact address of her destination—and most important:
c. believed the instructions.

She hears reproof in the recorded voice: "When safe, make a U-turn," which leaves the phrase, "you fool!" unstated but clearly implied. There is also the slight problem of believing her errant sense of direction, to the point of having no doubt, on one occasion, that a college prankster had turned the street signs to fool unsophisticated drivers. That trip took a bit longer.

And so she heads off on another adventure, in the ever optimistic mindset of gaining the prize she seeks, and still making the next appointment on time. But timeliness is a topic for another day.

THE BEST

The best is the morning hour of sleep gifted to me by my bedmate who silently goes about her morning rituals, tiptoeing around my rest.

The best is breakfast at Lots of Lox, where "the usual" is understood by all to be eggs and onions done not too dry or too loose, with tomatoes and dry rye toast. It means hello from all, a discussion of the latest sports event with Jimmy, the owner, or the latest school challenge of Laurie, the waitress who was tutored by my wife before beginning pre-nursing courses.

The best is the hour at the gym being multi-virtuous, reading and moving the stationary bicycle nowhere, while my imagined fitness soars.

The best is the ninety minutes in writing class, submitting the workings of my imagination to praise and suggestion and criticism; then doing the same for the remarkably honest and delightful group of retirees I call classmates and friends.

The best is the silent hour wrested from the day to explore the computer, research whatever my mind no longer recalls or never knew and may not remember.

The best time of day is the late afternoon when I lie in bed with my beloved, while thunder rolls through endless canyons unseen.

The best is dinner with friends—last minute is fine—no pretense, just real faces coming to relax and decompress and share.

The best is being invited into the living room to make it whole, as my sweetheart and I share *our show.*

The best is the warmth that awaits me in bed and how she lights the way at night with her glowing watch so I don't trip, and gently welcomes me back though I have interrupted her sleep.

The best is driving to the destinations of a lifetime knowing she is beside me, a lover, a mother, a guardian, a friend.

THE OPTIMIST MARRIES
THE PESSIMIST

I am a pessimist by nature and training. The first lesson in medical school besides *primum non nocere*—first do no harm—is to treat for the most dangerous and immediate illness. That means *always* thinking of the worst and leaving denial at home. Having this background that did not forgive or tolerate mistakes, I learned early to focus on all that could possibly go awry. I specialized more and more until my area of expertise was one organ system, the lungs. That way I could know most of what could go wrong in my limited sphere.

My wife Marilyn was encouraged and supported in all things as a girl. It was okay for her to start a project which even if not finished, would be greeted with praise and encouragement. This early imprinting led to a life of exploration including weaving, handicrafts, sewing, making bread dough plaques, knitting, creating works of art from doll house doors and windows. It led to trying new careers including computer programming, teaching middle school, managing a medical office, opening a gift store, teaching high school biology, managing another medical office and running the local office for the re-election of America's first black president. She fearlessly introduced the Secretary of the Treasury, Jack Lew and Senator Al Franken to a burgeoning roomful of the faithful.

Perhaps it was my experience in college of being so late handing in papers that I spent the hour of the class writing the last page then rushing in as class ended to present my work. Perhaps it was being overwhelmed with patient responsibility when I got a slow start early in my internship. Whatever the cause, I found the safest route to inner calm was to be early. Even today I list reasons why we should allow an extra hour at the airport, thirty minutes more to drive to Broward or even 15 minutes to cross US1: there could be road construction, an accident, a presidential entourage blocking off the Palmetto, car trouble, a need to use the bathroom at one of the fast food places en route or phone calls that may delay our departure *if we don't leave NOW.*

Marilyn is ever the optimist, "Traffic will be fine." She often tries to get one more thing done before we leave. She believes that getting to a friend's house early can be rude, for who expects guests to be on time? She humors me by planning our departure to the minute, allocating the estimated time needed for each task before leaving. Somehow driving time is rarely mentioned, as if we will beam ourselves across US1.

We are often late.

ON FOLDING A WHITE LAUNDRY

A LOVE STORY

I admire the whiteness and clean scent as they emerge from the dryer. Static electricity making dirigibles of her silky smooth ones that balloon and seem ready to float away. They crackle to the touch and settle back to two dimensional softness. Their neighbors reach up to communicate and share electrons, releasing all tension as they nestle as one until needed.

Their whiteness illuminates the room, their freshness radiates. His, stack like soldiers on dress parade in perfect alignment, each identical to the one below as if they drilled for hours to attain such precision. But nearby is a touch of color nearly concealed within the whiteness. Clinging with the electric attraction that melds two entities into one, the silkiness of the stow away is detected. I get the motivation, though I am barely able to imagine what goes on in the wooden chest when the lights go out. But being the keeper of order and the resident adult I must separate by sex, though my sympathies lie with the bold attempt.

Those irascible socks are at it again. Having no loyalty they leave their mates at first opportunity. Once again we sound the general alarm and would turn on the strobe lights if we had any, for one is missing. All hands on deck as we illuminate every possible hiding place. Got the craven cur, found curled up in a dark corner of the dryer hoping we wouldn't notice. This isn't our first rodeo, cowboy. Back in line with the other shoe-dwellers.

We fold together as our lives are enfolded. We stack as the years have compiled, one on the next. And we laugh at things made funnier because our partner finds it so. Each doing a part, we strive to make our share more than half. She lifts when I can't. I go up stairs knowing her knees will protest.

Anticipation is an art perfected through a common history and caring and love. You need not rush off to slay dragons or conquer empires to prove dedication. It is there in the simple act of two people folding white laundry, as one.

AND MARRIAGE

THANKSGIVING

How sweet to see my son and daughter
Chatting happily, engaging
Remembering a joined past,
Sharing lives today and years ago.

The grandsons like magnetic poles
Seek each other, bound by electronics
Inseparable, for a while,
So special is the sleep-over.

The older ones, now young adults
Take longer to part the curtain
Dividing young male and female-ness
To reveal the kids they were.

The guitar rarely rests, as the son-in-law
Plays rhythms learned this week.
The seventeen year old plays any tune
The internet informs, and well.

The women, my women, the grandma/wife
The daughter/mother, the sweet in-laws
Seek patterns for a sewing project
And the irresistible Home Goods nearby.

We plan a run, my son and I
To meet his son at MIA.
A college man now, a man
With classes he doesn't miss.

They visit two families; I don't begrudge.
For Thanksgiving is sweetest
In the quiet time when molecules collide
And meld to re-form our solar system.

ANTICIPATION

The tables are set, the taco meat simmering on the stove. After three shopping forays all the ingredients are accounted for. New teal colored plastic cups have been purchased to match the plates. The lettuce and tomatoes have been reduced to acceptable slivers so they can easily slide into taco shells, standing in anticipatory stacks. Green and glowing, the guacamole awaits. Crispy chocolate chip cookies sit expectantly alongside the two boxes of black and white cookies, a perennial favorite of the kids soon to arrive from Tennessee. Dried fruit slices await the vegans in the group. Their local cousins will soon be here, hungry for reunion and good food.

We, the grandparents atingle with barely suppressed excitement, channeled into preparations upon preparations. The food is ready. The table is set. Two magic tricks have been practiced and the set-ups are on the living room table to peak curiosity before "the show." There is time for a shower, a supreme sign of successful planning.

The two eighteen-year-olds, my grandson and a friend already here, will be awakened at 12:30p.m., allowing enough time to get ready before the onslaught of relatives. Wait, sounds from upstairs; the grandson and friend are up. They went to a late movie, 'The Purge 2'. Now is the time for purging sleep with a wake-up shower. The house is coming alive.

Let the wild rumpus begin!

THEIR UNIVERSE

I savor the texture of each
Morsel that is their lives.
The mountain-top home in the pure cool air.

The movement within, an intricate dance
How they mesh and bounce off
As orbits intersect collide,

Separate, brush by, erupt.
Drawn and repelled by the gravity
Of brothers they flow through the day

Separated by dark matter,
Emerging with age and change,
Closed doors and moods

From which no light escapes,
To preserve the space required
For expansion of each.

One soon to be a comet,
Breaking from his ellipse.
So comfortable, so known

Seeking other worlds, while still
Including family in
The new universe he explores.

Like Zeus, the father,
He sets the order
Of this Olympic home.

Days and nights he never fails
To be a rock, the nucleus
Defining physical laws,

Making sense of chaos
Making stable the sand
That could swallow

One less watchful.

The mother: like electrons
She flickers between,
Making equal the energy,

Discharging the current before
Spark begets lightning and thunder.
She brings a gentle order

To the random forces circling
About, in rings upon rings
Held by the pull of her

Goodness and love.

THE COMMITMENT

At the seventh hour of the seventh day of the seventh week her commitment has been met, a commitment to principle, to self, to another. Her office, the dining room table, covered in chronologically deposited evidence of her labor. At one end she hunches over the Mac until her torso demands stretching. Surrounded by call lists—those to be called, those who have been, those who will be again—she directs the cyber-pestering, a blend of new and old that defines the persuasion of a political campaign. Papers that back up the back-up for the temperamental program, which like a night club bouncer gone awry, ejects the faithful at random moments. On each print out—sorted by geography, disbursed, and alphabetically coded—are those who will call, or who will call those who will call.

On one side is the endless diet Coke, gift of the Gods to the driven who's other commitment is to a Tuesday weigh in. Across are left over tea cups or a salad container lined with dressing now separated into the immiscible components, not unlike the voters she calls upon. The far reaches hold unread mail, magazines and the clothing being gathered for the post election escape. The air, cooled to maximize focus, creates a light mist on the living room windows.

Her mood—concentration mixed with fatigue, stirred by computer driven anxiety and urgency to complete the task of Sisyphus—always upbeat, political piecework delivered with a velvet glove, "Hi, I'm Marilyn with the Obama campaign. I'm so proud to see that you volunteered to ..." "Meet at 10 AM at..." "Bring a cell phone. Don't forget to turn your clock back one hour tonight." Social service is added when an unrecorded human voice answers. "Oh, you do sound so ill. Try hot tea with lemon and maybe you can make calls later in the week." "You're Dad! Oh my gosh. I'm so sorry. I hope he gets out soon. Maybe you can still get him an absentee ballot." " A break in! It took how many hours for the police to come? Thank God you weren't home. Don't feel guilty; you've done more than your share already."

Three to four hours twice a day this labor of choice, of duty, of patriotism is repeated as cheerfully as humanly possible. The computer says she made 1430 calls. She laughs and equates this accuracy with other data spewed by this electronic prevaricator. By the end of shift, while still upbeat, she sags as the phone and her energy disconnect.

Between shifts she clings to *538*, a website which puts our team in the 80% range for favorable outcome, predictions that are flotation in the political storm.

Life is scheduled around the calls, the endless calls. Friends are greeted "Hi I'm Marilyn, oops you know that." Call backs intrude on the (un)free time. Always in her mind is the need to check in with the 19-year-old supervisor, Occidental College student, getting credit for applied political science.

The effectiveness of her efforts is seen one Saturday when our home becomes the node, the decentralized meeting place. From 8 a.m. to 7 p.m. we greet, train, feed, and attend to fluid needs of ten pairs of canvassers. They go in pairs, many strangers. The goal, to get your side to vote early, make a commitment. Visit one and the percent voting will increase. Set a time for them to vote and the percentage increases yet again. Sign a pledge to vote and you got 'em, all worked out by others years before. They return four hours later with a satisfied fatigue, arranging luncheon dates with their newfound friends. First a debriefing, house by house report of those met, those absent, those targeted for a revisit or call. All the while cell phones work as the lady from California and local volunteers, many retired, search for the less committed.

With faith in the planners, the predictors, the pundits they push on. It worked in '08 didn't it? Would they tell us if Florida was lost?

So she labors, believing, hoping the most recent *538* forecast could be wrong. "Pink is so close to light blue. Maybe one more call...." Is the last thought as sleep can no longer be denied.

WE SHARE

We have grown together like vines wrapped so tightly they could be taken for one. In the decades we have chosen to share, our tastes have often merged, melded. We share a taste for tea after dinner, a sense of what is a desirable room temperature, a respect for each other's opinion on matters of import.

We share tasks out of fairness, and appreciation and duty and love. A bed made by two is a gift to each other, and a statement, and a promise.

We share memories of a life and the wondrous products of that life. We are an extension of each other's memory—an enhancement adding depth to each experience. We can enjoy a movie even more when it reminds us of one in our collective archive. And we smile at the joint recognition, the journey into our common past merging into our present.

We share warmth as the morning light emerges and one returns to bed, chilled by the cool night air and needing a warm connection, revitalization, transfusion—warmth a most basic unit of support.

We share days, we share nights, we share meals and treats that make us glow. We share concerns for each other. If one is affected, the other feels it, for discontent, like laughter is contagious. Our futures like our pasts are woven together, with hopes and dreams and fears fused into one sculpted vision, which we have pledged to share. Our word is good, for that we also share.

THE GARAGE
ON STOWING THE PAST AND
FUTURE

The passage through our garage each day is a journey through history, unnoticed in the rush to the urgent present or to future planning. This room of leftovers houses pieces of my life, each glimpse a portal to deeper memories—a three dimensional photo album.

The artifacts recall my father-in-law whose rusty tools repaired everything from the washing machine to the TV wiring he designed and installed, and only he could modify. On a high shelf my father's 16mm projector sits idle, the films of my childhood long since converted to digital tape, then to CD's. Next to his is my 8 mm projector which has seen our honeymoon as we climbed the dunes of Cape Cod, seen my children as infants nestled in hospital blankets within one arm of an astoundingly young looking intern/father, seen the milestones of these children as they grew to join the ranks of insecure young parents. By the time their children grew, new equipment had long eclipsed the shelved relics gathering dust here—but in no danger of disposal, for who would discard their past?

The work bench stands, ignominiously storing "stuff" that doesn't fit elsewhere, like the dusty library stacks at Brooklyn College, where I met the girl who would share my life, my memories, our garage. That work bench (or was it the predecessor?) provided the platform for constructing the bookshelves, looking like a doll house, we made for my daughter's room when her scattered books made the room unnavigable. A similar shelving unit followed two years later for my son, this one looking like a locomotive. Like the work bench, these two had long ago lost utility and had been banished or retasked.

There is an enlarged photo of my wife, my favorite photo to this day. We are in Grindlewald, Switzerland, hiking and she slipped crossing a stream soaking her boot and sock. The picture is of her crossing the icy stream, barefoot, with a huge smile on her face—her spirit and resilience captured on a glossy print, blown up to poster size for all to see at her 40th birthday party.

The Coleman lantern which illuminated many overnight adventures looks down upon me from on high. That lantern attracted moths which entertained the baby who is now into early middle age and hosts a gala 70th birthday party for her father, making it seem effortless. That lamp helped show us the way to our station wagon at 3 am when our canvas tent began to leak in a rain storm because the amateur campers forgot to place a plastic tarp under the tent, and didn't even know the term 'entrench'.

To one corner lies the box filled with gambling paraphernalia such as chips, and blackjack table cloths. The first party held in our pre-hurricaned house—so revealing of the character of the attendees. One newly married couple, each rebounding from divorce, were seen to meticulously keep their money from touching, though the hundred dollar bills had my picture on them and the ones, a photo of my dog.

The old tool box that held fishing tackle now rusts uncomplaining next to the projectors. That box was at my side when I took my son and daughter fishing under the Card Sound Bridge. My son, with the perfected stubbornness of an eight year old, wanted to go past the walkway and onto the concrete support abutment to fish. To avoid ending the day on a note of confrontation, I went along, my daughter sensibly hanging back. After baiting his rod, and handing it back to him, I was putting a worm on my hook when something hit me in the head. It was his rod. "What the..." I began to say to my son who was no longer there. He had fallen in. I searched in near panic for what seemed like minutes but must have been fractions of that, when he resurfaced on the left of where I had guessed. I grabbed him, pulled him out and took a soaking wet son and crying daughter, who was convinced she had just witnessed her brother drowning, home. We never again fished from the Card Sound Bridge.

The cabinets that line our garage have doors, pierced with nails from which hang our "art". We have attended *Wine and Design,* a fun painting class for amateurs, facilitated by wine and snacks, where the instructor breaks down an Everglades sunset, or picture of Buddha or a collage of an elephant. We step-by-step through the basic geometry to discover, always a surprise, a unique creation accomplished enough to hang in our home; in this case in the garage. There are 16 such pictures, the last having been created a few days ago along with our out of town friends who joined us at a pre-birthday paint fest. Their works of art will all be kept at their homes; it will be interesting to see if that means the garage.

Our future is well represented by a line of furniture taking up nearly the length of one side of the garage, destined for Asheville and our new summer home. End tables that held a grandmother's memories have been lovingly refinished. A dresser—which saw the marriage of that girl adorned Grandma's house during her 50-year marriage and accompanied her widowed years as she moved in with her daughter, my mother-in-law—will now adorn the house of the third generation. String lights await the patio as do the barbecue tools which precede the grill.

An archeologist could make much of this modest room. At least five generations revealed amid the trash and treasure we refuse to discard, including my daughter's uncashed Bat Mitzvah check discovered in this same garage 25 years after the event.

THE FIGHT

Round 1:   5 p.m.—Marilyn states that there is a David Sedaris course that she would like to take, and the teacher is Lisa Reyes; she looks the question, and finally verbalizes it: would it be all right? I shake my head no—slowly and not without thought, nor without selfishness—for the realm of non-fiction writing has been mine. I have vested my interest, my energy, my ego, as I have tried to reinvent myself from a stiff formal physician to a persona of wit, wisdom and having a facility with words, or so I tell myself. I enjoy the class, the people in it and the teacher. I look forward to it and mold vacations around it. When people ask *The* question: "So what do you *DO* now that you don't work?" my answer is," I write." In truth, I also attend an investment class which is enjoyable as a snack but not a sustained diet, and have taken two courses on line, poetry and economics, as well as a *Great Courses* offering, *How to Write Great Sentences.* The course that sustains my interest, where I belong, is writing and I'm afraid of losing that. Marilyn is very funny and bright and has great recall of humorous events despite the usual noun-misplacement that occurs on many 65th birthdays. I am concerned about her superior skills, especially in the realm of humor. I am in essence afraid of being shown up, unmasked as the poseur that I am.

Round 2: 6p.m.—I try to talk about it and she initially refuses but does own up to "I'm mad at you." I proffer a compromise percolating in my guilt center: an email to Lisa Reyes, the instructor, asking if this is a lit. course or a writing one, thinking that Marilyn would opt for the former but not the latter. I get her to converse enough to recognize the attempt at compromise but also to elicit that she would want to be in either class. Problem continues to simmer.

Round 3: 6:30p.m.—I hear her making food in the kitchen but she neither consults me as to dinner choices, nor informs me of her choice, nor invites me to participate. Ouch, that was the sound of the gauntlet being dropped—on my foot.

Round 4: The roller ball is now in my court. I can go out to dinner without telling her, leaving quietly so she won't even know I've gone, a strategy that is sure to inflame, or I can tell her I am going to a bring in food—"Would you like some?"—knowing full well that she has just eaten something far less appealing than what I am offering. Ha! The latter emphasizes my consideration, while drawing a stark contrast with her selfish, uncommunicative whipping up of unshared tuna. Since there are extenuating circumstances, she has a back injury and has been taking prednisone, known to be mood-altering; I choose the high road, if Chicken Kitchen can even vaguely be considered the high road to anything other than indigestion. She at first doesn't hear me with earphones in place. *Or does she?* "Would you like me to bring anything back for you? I ask without sarcasm, the killing-with-kindness counter offensive in operational mode. With a pained expression she requests a quarter-dark chicken. Unsaid is, "Where were you when I made the tuna?" (How could I know that tuna was being made since I wasn't invited to participate? Hee, hee).

Round 5: 7:30PM—Went to *Chicken Kitchen,* placed my order and in a spiteful mood—for even the killing-them-with-kindness approach has its limits—did not object, as she usually does, when pita is placed on the platter. Home in no time and without saying a word, I set two placemats on the cocktail table in front of the TV and serve the dinner with napkins, silver ware and her favorite beverage, diet coke. No word of thanks is offered. She turns off season 2 of *Veronica Mars* and puts on the evening news, a clear concession to my prefer-ences, sans communication. Then in mid-broadcast she wordlessly clears her plate and goes upstairs. To be fair the news had so much destruction and mayhem that I too wanted to flee. I debate showing her this essay as a way of humorously defusing the tension, then come to my senses. This will be viewed as mocking and will be the gasoline on the smoldering flames, creating a tear-ful meltdown, *and she may cry also.* Time is the salve and when the wound is no longer inflamed then the splin-ter will be removed—though I know that this approach is rarely effective in medicine or marital spats. We will probably both tire of this and each insist on giving in. But not tonight.

Round 6: 11:20 p.m.—I did the TV instead of going to bed thing. This makes it more likely that I'll sleep in the guest bedroom, *so as not to wake Marilyn.* Seems like a generous thing to do since she sometimes has problems getting back to sleep, except if you examine what I was watching, *Parenthood,* a TV equivalent of infidelity since we always watch *Parenthood* together. Angry TV watching pattern, plus angry bedtime behavior portends longer time interval needed until anger blows over.

Round 7: 11:40p.m.—I sneak upstairs with my New Balances in my hand so as to minimize the staircase creaks. I even skip step #2 to avoid the loud crack that has been there for the past month. Silently drop sneak-ers in closet, go into bathroom with all lights out and by the shower light take my meds and soundlessly—and I mean Indian-sneak-attack silently—creep into the hallway, and don't even turn out staircase light until the bedroom door is oh so slowly closed, because the change may awaken her. I open the guest bedroom door and turn on the light and BAZINGA!!! There she is asleep in the guest room. Check mate. She beat me to it and I awakened her with the light. A quinella. Brilliant countermove I must concede. Both referees and the judge give round 7 to Marilyn. Well played.

Round 8: 9:30 a.m. March 27, 2014—the next morning. I slept late, unawakened by Marilyn's movements, her side of the bed pristine, unused. I hear her TV down the hall, her door open. I open my door and turn on the TV. The positions set, all that is missing is the music from *High Noon*, as we face off not knowing who will make the first move, who will flinch, who will show weakness. As Gary Cooper minus the gun belt—and minus pants if you must know—I swagger down the hall and enter the guest bedroom, all amnesia and light. "So how's your back? Did you sleep well?" The answers are direct and brief, formal, neither warm nor cold—the tone of the day yet to be declared. Then a bold move: she ventures into a new area of conversation and says "I dropped my I-pad" then further details offered without the need of my probing, "I think I'll have to take it into the store. It's not working"—a generous offering of information, spontaneously given. Is it a test? Should I jump in to help? What's to lose? I offer to look at the injured appendage; could a doctor do less? It remains dormant, depriving me of a defrosting opportunity. But then in a last-ditch act of desperation I remove it from the protective casing that has nearly fused with the shell and with one final thrust am able to insert the power cord far enough to generate that discordant tone signifying contact, electrical union. Could this heal the damage, right the wrong, calm the disturbance in the Force? I leap up the stairs to report the breakthrough. The news is met with a luke-warm reception, her eyes unwavering from the TV screen, another attempt at Glasnost on the rocks.

Round 9: 10:15 a.m.—Marilyn is downstairs and pronounces the I-pad unimproved. "I'm going to the *Apple* store, (Exclusive of me, I guess.) after breakfast."(Inclusive of me? A sign of thawing?) "If you want to come." (Asking if I am still angry?) Then she adds," I'll take my own car." (So much for thawing.)

Round 10: Lots of Lox Restaurant, 10:30 a.m.— She is doing the crossword puzzle, intent, not looking up. I say, "What does the puzzle title mean?" And a conversation starts, a real more-than-one-word answer conversation. Bless you Will Shortz and your Sunday *New York Times* crossword. You have provided a DMZ where the combatants can disarm and re-establish diplomatic relationships. We even chat together/separately with our waitress and Nick, one of the owners. Barriers being deconstructed as we leave, both deciding for a stop at home before our separate future destinations, mine the gym, hers the Apple store. I check my email and see that Lisa has answered that the course is a writing course. This might make it easier for Marilyn to bow out but clearly in negotiations as delicate as these, timing is everything. This is not the time to throw a potentially incendiary device into the slowly forming re-engagement. I make a strategic decision to withhold this critical bit of information until a more propitious time. The ground must be more fertile before planting this seed for even the most hardy plant will not take root in frozen earth. Off to a neutral corner, the YMCA gym.

Round 11: 1:50 p.m.—The time away has been salutary. The I-pad was not irreparably damaged, just needed a prolonged two button push to reset its traumatized neuro-network. I had stopped and picked up 12 volt batteries for M's garage door opener but found I could make it work by cleaning off the contacts and bending them so that contact was firm. Two successes between us and the air turbulence had calmed to a gentle breeze. Time for a shower and then perhaps lunch, perhaps with a friend who might lighten the mood further? I'll call. Arrrggggh. Too late. Marilyn just had a guacamole snack and is not up for lunch. Back still a bother, so she may lie down. This may have to run its course with no obvious fast track to happiness in sight.

But no, a change of heart, she will have a Greek salad, no olives, no onions as take out. I bring it home after having my salad at a leisurely pace at the restaurant. She has the salad while watching *Veronica Mars* episode 4,026, ear phones on, communication off. Then: "Do you want tea?" she offers. "Do you want Tylenol?" I counter. Bonding with items beginning with the letter T is a very good sign. I don't push onward to S as in Seat cushion, Sugar or Smores.

Round 12:   7:45 p.m.—I show Marilyn this essay and.........

REMNANTS

The first hint that our neighborhood had been destroyed came with the evening news, showing the National Guard setting up armed outposts in our local shopping center. We were 700 miles north at a Sleep Medicine-1992 conference, trying unsuccessfully to call friends in Miami-Dade county, or what was left of it. We finally reached a nephew in Broward who said: "Come home *now*." He strongly suggested we fly into Ft. Lauderdale, rent a car and buy some plastic, a stapler, nails and basic tools. My wife asked: "Could we use tape instead, since we don't want to make permanent holes in the wood?" I could hear, *soto voce*, in the muffled receiver, "I don't think she quite understands what's happened."

The drive South down US1 was a gradual descent into Hurricane Hell. Signs were grotesquely twisted, or missing glass, or missing. What was that mangled lot filled with downed trees and trash? Together we gasped when its true identity was unmasked as the remainder of a lovely wayside park with the lake replaced by debris. We had the time in which to orient as the traffic crawled in the absence of electric powered signals. The one dangling traffic light defined SW 152 St. We turned east but had to drive slalom around fallen trees, which took us up the rutted lawns of several houses. Our street, shorn of foliage, was unrecognizable; we drove past twice before counting the blocks from the park and turning in disbelief. A neighbor had cleared the obstructions that used to be lovely shade trees, using heavy equipment borrowed from his construction company.

Our home stood with its doors blown open and all the windows gone. My wife said, "There's some good plywood we can use," pointing to our front yard. Then we realized there were shingles on the other side. We were looking at our roof.

Pebbles of glass coated everything as if an indoor hail storm descended and refused to melt. No room was pardoned. The wooden living room floor buckled like a moguled ski run. The kitchen showed blades of saw grass stuck like throwing knives into the wooden door frame. Pantry doors appeared to be spared until opened, revealing two inches of salt water on every shelf.

I turned to find my wife vigorously cleaning off glass and debris from a small round circle of the kitchen counter in a futile effort to impose order somewhere, anywhere. Tears were reserved for the dining room. There was a large bowl filled with photos, which captured our life's most precious moments—fused into a solid lump; drowned by a thief named Andrew, who stole our lives in a few short hours.

Trying to separate the pictures only separated parts of each from its mounting paper. Even the framed wedding picture was a hazy fusion of the past now partly residing on the glass. Of all we lost that day, these pieces that meant the most, were uninsured—the remnants of our past.

⊷⊰⊱⊶

Engrossed in the effort of regathering a life, we spent months superficially ordering what used to be a thing of comfort and beauty while living in a camper in the front yard. The glass beads were gathered, shelves drained of standing water, our rabbit buried in the alcove where he lived. Weeks became months before the insurance adjuster came through. "This is a beautiful house," he said. "It was," I answered. "It *is*," he persisted gently. "Well, let's hope it will be again," I compromised; and even won a bet that there was something that he had never seen before. "I've seen it all," he replied; then added, "Well, that's new!" after seeing my dress shoes covered in grey fungus, as if an inch of dust had settled and stuck. He wrote a big check on the spot and said that more was coming as the repair estimates came in.

Like the immovable layer on my shoes, sadness settled and would not be cleansed, especially when we saw the bonded block of pictures we could not bear to remove from the dining room. The photo store reframed the wedding picture, at our insistence, but its luster was gone as if Andrew had personally sanded off all the joy.

We watched as the tree fragments were relocated to the sidewalks and carted off by FEMA trucks. Blue visqueen patches became a solid roof. The roller coaster living room floor became shiny ... and flat, and new. Room by room the house revived, but like a death in the family a hollow place remained, unfilled by new sheetrock or shingle.

The missing piece arrived in a plain brown package. Our lifelong friends, layered through our past like frosting through a cake, had duplicated photos of our joined history in an album: the vacations, the celebrations, the street signs showing our way home. The hole in our hearts was patched, the remnants of our life restored.

MEDICAL TRAINING

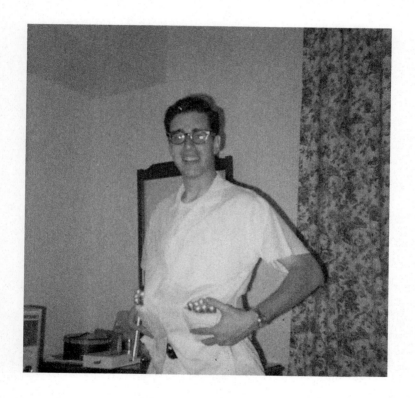

ACCEPTING DEATH

"You will each have *at least* one cardiac arrest." There is an audible murmur of nervous laughter followed by sober acceptance among the group of 20 somethings that comprise my first year medical school class. The first step in dealing with death and dying is to accept its inevitability not for them but for us, for me. The exercise is to write our own obituary.

There is more muffled joking by the mostly male class about being done in at a ripe old age by a jealous husband. Humor fades as we explore the myriad ways of exiting life and if our inheritance would define them. We carry the genes of our parents and grandparents. Along with their eye color and height they have shared cholesterol levels and a tendency for the nuclear mishaps that convert perfectly normal cells to ones with unrestrained growth and metastasis. Silence now fills the room as we contemplate the inevitable chinks in our armor that will result in the submission of a real obituary.

The first sentence is the most difficult, establishing on paper the fact of what is to come and on a date certain in the unknowable future. To a person, we seek reassurance by choosing a time far in the future, though we know it is an optimistic fiction. The uncertainty of that time is the second sobering fact absorbed that morning. We could be unlucky. We could succumb to the sudden traumatic end of young risk takers in a swerving car or ski off a poorly marked trail in Zermatt. More chilling is the randomness of a routine blood test result revealing the primitive cells that define leukemia or any of the mine field of fatal maladies that fill the texts we so recently bought.

It may not be our fault. It may be bad luck on a grand scale, a thought that pauses my pen as the possibility is approached, cautiously circumnavigated and finally accepted in all its unfairness. Probability defines much of life and so I take comfort in statistics. A comet may have ended the dinosaurs but my end will much more likely be willingly ingested as the traditional fare that constricts vital arteries. *Death by chopped liver* brings a mildly amused smile, how fitting, how logical, how probable. Colon cancer has taken two of my father's sibs—so many organ systems, so many ways to go wrong. My ignorance of pathology shields me from more disquieting paths to the grave.

I, of course, will leave behind many loving children and theirs, each independent and on a path ensuring success, however that be defined. The date, so far in the future will involve a person I no longer recognize.

We initiates will in whatever field we choose, deal with the process of death. Most often it will be distressing, whether sudden or gradual; sometimes welcomed by the sufferer, but felt by those remaining as a loss frequently suffused with guilt. The care givers we are to become will share all of these feelings plus the nagging sense that this outcome could have been prevented if we were better at our chosen profession.

And so we are introduced to the ultimate outcome which we can at best delay. By this simple exercise the lesson is taught that all life is borrowed, not given, even our own.

MY FIRST PATIENT

I felt like a fraud as I approached my first patient.

The Medical College of Virginia believed in patient contact as early as the first year of medical school. I arrived having just turned twenty and looking closer to sixteen, in one of the three required sport jackets bought for seven dollars each on sale at Wallach's in Brooklyn. My skinny tie, knotted tightly, made my thin neck with bulging veins resemble that of a chicken being strangled. Our first year included a Saturday morning course, Man and His Environment, which was in part an introduction to physical diagnosis, genetics, psychiatry and especially a reminder that we were treating people with families and not organ systems.

By the end of the first year we had sufficient knowledge of a rudimentary history and physical to try them out on stable but nonetheless chronically ill patients at the McGuire VA Hospital. The economics of the time required VA hospitals to fill all their beds or lose some. This meant that prolonged hospitalizations were not discouraged. Many vets lived for months in the VA as their chronic illnesses were treated. One of the sometimes unwelcome diversions from the monotony of VA existence was the arrival of a new batch of medical students, once again taking an endlessly detailed medical history and physical often lasting hours.

The day came for my foray into the world of diagnostic medicine. Once before on a hospital tour, I had borrowed a white jacket and walked with a fourth year student through the emergency room waiting area. Every step I took was tracked by dozens of pairs of eyes. I wanted to apologize, to say, "Don't worry, I'm not the one you are waiting for. I'm not the magic healer, not yet, if ever." So much was projected on the wearer of the white coat; I was embarrassed at the implied deception, the feeling that I was letting them down. I wanted to explain but just kept walking like the older student, pretending not to notice the attention. Had he been rendered immune to it by repeated exposure or just not caring?

I was fortified by a book listing the endless elements of a complete history and physical exam, or H&P, and my new Lederle medical bag with stethoscope, reflex hammer and tuning fork. These tools of the trade had been the gift of a drug company which had also provided an all expenses paid weekend in New York for my entire class, an acceptable practice in 1965. I clung to the bag as tightly as Batman to his mask, hoping the disguise would hide the insecure mortal beneath.

I was led with several of my classmates to a first floor ward in a chronic care area of the hospital. It was a large nearly square open room housing at least twenty men. Faded white metal beds, with grate-like headboards resting against pale government green walls, the feet pointing to their opposite numbers across the room. Each bed had an adjacent small metal table for the personal effects of the patient and was isolated by curtains when privacy was required. The overall impression was bland to the point of indifference. It was cold and devoid of personal effects, giving the feeling of being rented by its occupants but not owned. Some beds were filled with patients attached to tubes, adding or subtracting body fluids. Some walked around in the blue robes and pajamas, their new uniforms, off to smoke or the bathroom or to change scenery.

I was shown my patient by a resident who promptly left. I pulled up a heavy gray Government Issue metal chair and introduced myself, careful not to utter the unearned title, *Doctor.* The patient in his 50s was a thick bodied grizzled veteran of many battles, some I'm certain involving a barroom." I'm Paul Gustman a first year—" I never got to finish as he interrupted in booming tones which could be heard throughout the ward and I feared in neighboring counties. "I HAVE MILIARY TUBERCULOSIS," he roared, "THAT'S M-I-L-I-A-R-Y," slowly attacking each letter, louder than the last, ending in a virtual shout. My face reddened with the knowledge that every eye in the place was on him/us. I felt each letter as a sledgehammer pounding me ever lower in my seat. All disguise was stripped away by the intentional mocking of my inexperience. Thankfully the jacket restrained most of the sweat welling from my every pore. His performance completed and exasperation vented at dealing with yet another unwanted interruption of his day, the rest of the exam was uneventful and in conversational tones. He was likeable in the manner of my gruff uncles and more cooperative than I deserved.

It was my first lesson in trying to view the world from the perspective of another; getting through defenses, not reacting to them. How would I feel being indefinitely incarcerated in such a drab room, with minimal privacy and interruptions for the sole benefit of others?

I was the new initiate being knowledgeable of nothing, not disease, treatment, or even hospital decorum. I had a lot to learn, though I never forgot how to spell *M-I-L-I-A-R-Y.*

ER CRUCIBLE

A third year medical student has far more theoretical knowledge than practical, a fact that became humbling in the spring of 1968 during my first month in the emergency room. Along with a white coat we were given the empty honorific of *Doctor*, without any of the experience that imbues the title with meaning; young scrubbed faces trying to appear competent to the patients, all the while sensing that we didn't know what we didn't know. Duties initially were limited to following a fourth year student around, he reporting to an intern, who reported to a resident, who had all manner of consultants to call upon if needed including the ER director, a dynamic well respected and demanding South African physician, whose gentle smile could evaporate should incompetence be detected.

In theory this was a reinforced construction, melding high quality medical care for the indigent with medical education through immersion. The carefully constructed lattice of supervision crumbled on the days when the volume of patients overwhelmed the providers and anyone with a stethoscope, teamed with an ER nurse, saw sick people as fast as possible. *Treat 'em and street 'em* was the ethos and the marching orders. Backup by a more experienced physician was obtained only if the medical student recognized the need for help. Sometimes he didn't.

I was two weeks into a month-long rotation in the medical ER. This was real medicine, real people with real disease. I had done a fair job of triage, treating those I could and asking for help at appropriate times. This led to an increasing level of trust from the fourth year student and the supervising intern. They were busy enough so that anyone who lightened the load was welcome, even a novice like me.

Late one afternoon I was called to see a haphazardly dressed woman in her forties who said she was having an asthma attack. I had treated several uncomplicated asthma patients in my brief time in the ER, following the recommendations of *The Manual of Medical Therapeutics*, the house staff bible seen bulging from the pockets of every white coat. This paperback salvation was specific, practical, and literally at hand when needed. It instructed that most asthma patients responded to inhalation therapy, the breathing in of medications that dilate the bronchial tubes, and injections of similar medicines given subcutaneously every twenty minutes. The nurse, a stern black woman of prodigious girth and experience, was concerned enough to direct me to see this lady first since respiratory emergencies wouldn't wait.

The patient sat in one of three *asthma chairs*, spoke in halting sentences, pausing between phrases to take in air and then musically release it much more slowly through pursed lips, as if she were trying to whistle. I could see that she was using her neck muscles to breathe and that her nasal openings flared with each breath, two signs of respiratory distress taught in our most basic physical diagnosis course. Her chest was an un-oiled gate. No stethoscope was needed to hear the loud diffuse wheezing. Haltingly she told of chronic asthma which had become worse when her young children shared a viral infection with her. She sat up wheezing all night and finally came to the ER when she could get someone to baby sit, many hours later.

Heeding *The Manual of Medical Therapeutics* to the letter, three inhalation treatments were given along with epinephrine injections, each at twenty minute intervals. I kept returning to listen to her chest while fitting in other patients with lesser illnesses. After an hour she was not complaining of symptoms. She said little. Wheezes were gone when I listened to her chest. Her heart rate and blood pressure were elevated, which I attributed to medication side effects. Her nasal passages no longer flared and neck muscles contracted less than on arrival, findings I naively took to mean improvement. Her apathetic facial expression was interpreted as the result of a sleepless night. In the opinion of this twenty-three year old inchoate *doctor*, she seemed well enough to be discharged from the ER.

I wrote discharge orders and prescriptions which were signed by the intern, who could not leave the bedside of a man having a heart attack. The nurse had a look of concern when she saw that my patient was being discharged. The patient, though sweating, was not visibly struggling to breathe and offered no complaint as she stood, staggered like a Saturday night drunk, mumbled incoherently and suddenly collapsed in the nurse's arms. Orderlies, recognizing a situation out of control, descended upon the scene and lifted the patient onto a stretcher. Like fighter pilots entering the fray, the entire ER staff gathered. The ER director himself shouldered his way through the crowd, sat the patient up and with well practiced movements did an abbreviated physical exam while talking to the patient. "She's not moving any air! Get respiratory therapy down here STAT! Get an IV going, aminophylline drip and a steroid bolus. "

I reached for the nearest blood pressure cuff, which in my brief time in clinical medicine proved to be a more reliable tourniquet to start IV fluids than the ubiquitous rubber tubing carried by all house staff physicians. The fourth year student who was supposed to be supervising me came over and yelled, "Get an IV going! Don't take her blood pressure!" I felt my face redden even more as I explained why I was using the cuff. The resident materialized and took over management which thankfully did not include life support. The patient eventually improved enough to be transferred to the ICU. Anger mixed with dread as I realized that I had nearly killed this woman, not out of malice but out of the ignorance of inexperience and was about to be taken to task for it.

The ER director eventually pulled me aside, along with several other students and discussed what went wrong. "Asthma," he pointed out "is caused by narrowing of the bronchial tubes. This causes turbulence of air and wheezing. When the airway narrowing is so severe that little air moves, then there is not enough airflow to create a wheeze. The listener thinks the resolution of wheezing is a sign of improvement when in fact it indicates worsening. This patient was moving so little air that her blood carbon dioxide level increased to the point of stupor. She was near death."

I felt his words like a slap, an indictment of my ineptitude and lack of supervision. "I've never seen such severe asthma before," was all I could offer. "I know," he said quietly. Then he gathered the interns and resident for a closed-door meeting, where his voice was not so restrained.

DISCONNECT

"Life should be preserved unless it becomes a burden to *both* the patient *and* the family." This philosophy had evolved in his four year medical school indoctrination and was soon to be tested. He was now taking one of his final electives before graduating with the Class of 1969, acting as an intern on the medical wards. Other than a slightly lighter load—8 patients instead of 12 for a 'real' intern—his duties and responsibilities were identical with those who actually possessed an MD degree. It was a heady taste of responsibility and authority. He could write orders that with few exceptions did not require co-signing. If procedures were needed—central lines, spinal taps, bone marrow aspirations—he did them all. He admitted and discharged. These were his patients and he was determined to provide the best care possible.

One patient discomfited him daily. She was a 62 year old woman who had suffered an intra-cerebral hemorrhage and was comatose. Her brain had stopped signaling the diaphragm to breathe and she was being kept alive by a Bird Respirator, a green plastic box connected to her airway by corrugated tubing. It had been so for weeks. Family, who had come and stayed around the clock initially, had been reduced to a daughter who came twice a week to spend 90 minutes holding her mother's hand, crying, and praying for a painless trip to the world beyond. Intra-family disagreements precluded any withdrawal of life support; with the relatives furthest away demanding—by phone, never appearing at bedside—that everything be done. "Only God can end a life," said the priest. She thanked him and asked him not to return.

The neurologists said there was massive brain damage which was irreversible. Neurosurgeons, usually more aggressive, concurred and wrote that surgical intervention would be ineffective and could well worsen the situation. Each day's rounds reiterated the futility of their efforts, which had been reduced to preventing bed sores, maintaining ventilation, nutrition and hydration; the latter three being delivered through their own tubes. At the point of entry, each tube had caused small skin erosions that oozed pink fluid.

Each day his anger grew at the useless effort which accomplished only the preservation of her suffering and that of her family. How inconceivable that the sum total of medical knowledge ill-served all involved. What was a physician's responsibility in such a situation? Was there a duty to provide futile care? Were not medical facilities a commodity to be husbanded and expended wisely for those who could benefit? Was this fair to patients who spent days on ER stretchers because this bed was filled with hopelessness?

Her plight violated all he believed about the healing arts. Was he doing good? No. Was he relieving suffering? No, he was prolonging it. Was he even giving hope—the last crumb when the larder was empty? Not a chance. Bound by a set of archaic rules demanding a course so totally wrong, he was frustrated and angry. No, anger was far too mild. He shook with the impotent rage of one observing a travesty, unable to intervene.

Finally on his night on call he decided to act. He was the only physician on the floor at 1AM when he went to her room. She was in an open ward with five other patients, each bed separated by off-white curtains, which he drew as silently as possible. He repeated the neurological exam for the hundredth time reconfirming that nothing had changed; no glimmer of hope had emerged. He then disabled the ventilator alarms and disconnected the ventilator tubing from the endotracheal tube in her airway. The rhythmic sound of air forced in and out of her lungs became a constant hiss of air never reaching the critical pressure to recycle. He stood there a full minute before quietly leaving her bedside, convinced he was doing the right thing. All was silent in the room but for the impotent leak of air beyond the curtain.

He went to the on call room nearby but could not sleep; unable to understand the malaise that descended upon him. He was doing what he believed was right. He could defend his action in his own court of judgment, of ethics, even of ultimate right….and wrong. Sleep came hours later, fitful and non-restorative.

Dread permeated his being as he awakened. What had he done? This was a life. Who was he to decide when it should end? What was he thinking? His first morning task was to enter her room and confirm that she had 'expired' during the night: to 'pronounce' his offense. He stopped midway, for he could hear it from the hall. It was unmistakable, the rhythmic sound of air being force in and then passively escaping from the lungs of one being ventilated. He had to hold on as he entered the room and there she was, reattached to the ventilator, unchanged, none the worse for his nighttime visit.

"Who did this?" he asked without uttering a sound: One of her roommates watching after a helpless lady? A nurse who happened by? An angel watching over patients cared for by the callow yet well intentioned? It didn't matter. His relief was total as he slowly exhaled his guilt. The weight of ending a life—so different than the theory of doing so—was gone. Had not shame choked his voice, he would have emitted a joyous shout, an exultation of sin expunged. Taking a life was not housekeeping. The Ten Commandments did not come with footnotes, not for him, not after the road of transgression he had traveled.

He still believed that life was worth preserving if it was of value to the patient or family. It was not the theory or theology, but the unbearable oppression and relief that swept over him the morning after, which guided his decisions for the next 40 years. Never again did he allow himself to be the sole arbiter of life's duration. He wasn't that willful, that cavalier, that foolish, or that strong.

THE KICK

An intern quickly learns that he is in the deep end of the pool, treading water as fast as he can to prevent drowning. This occurs before the strokes and the pace are refined, before efficiency streamlines each action. Tasks often descend in waves taking the form of admissions, sudden crises, procedures, and rounds, the seemingly endless reviews of patient care with those who know more and are charged with teaching through supervision of care.

As a medical student, one is on the periphery of the battle, observing, researching, but mostly not taking responsibility for the outcome. On July 1st following four years of preparation, trial by immersion begins. By a quirk of scheduling my first two months of internship were spent on electives with diminished responsibilities, rounding with subspecialty fellows. The first real ward responsibility began September 1969.

I assumed care for twelve people deemed too ill to live until their next clinic appointment, which was the unspoken admission criterion of the time. The other intern and I also admitted new patients every second night, each requiring more attention than the original twelve 'stable' people. The schedule was brutal, with 36 hours on and 12 hours off, and every second weekend on call. This meant that I would come to the hospital at 7 a.m. on Monday and be working with very little sleep if any until Tuesday at 5p.m. when the resident would chase me home. A weekend on call was even more challenging with continuous duties from Friday morning at 7a.m. until Monday night at 5 p.m. After one of the latter, I walked outdoors in my short sleeved intern's shirt for the first time in three days and after half a block realized I was knee deep in snow. Facing this schedule for the first time was daunting.

I would try to round on my inherited patients but never seemed to know them as well as the new admissions whom I interviewed in detail and for whom I formulated treatment plans. The hallway in E.G. Williams Hospital was long and at the end was one large room I never seemed to get to. Two patients there were seen mostly by medical students who didn't have the authority or knowledge to manage them properly. The occupants of the end room were mostly on "automatic pilot", the orders of the admitting intern, long departed. Each time I tried to get to that room events intervened, a new admission, a man ready for discharge who developed an acute GI bleed, a cardiac arrest. Medicine in such an environment is triage, which dictated low priority for the "stable."

In the desperate effort to stay afloat that was my first month on the ward, the last room became the end of the canoe accumulating water—a problem at first hidden but worse each day. Then came rounds with the assistant Chief of Medicine, a man I admired as one would a rock star. He was a superb clinician and a gentleman. He was such a dedicated researcher that he used himself as a subject for hypertension experiments where he placed arterial catheters in his arm for a 24-hour period and showed the remarkable variations in 'normal' blood pressure. He was cheerful, humorous, insightful—a paradigm to which we all aspired. I dreaded what was to come, my unmasking, my incompetence revealed. You could pretend to patients, feigning competence, but not to yourself and certainly not to the attending physician. As was the custom of the time we walked as a group from bed to bed, interns, a resident, medical students and the Assistant Chief. The intern would "present" the patient's pertinent history. The attending doctor would then introduce himself to the patient, ask a few questions and examine the patient. He would then move, with the rounding group, out of earshot of the patient and probe more deeply into the house staff's understanding of the medical issues, their plan for diagnosis and treatment. When my patients were discussed I went through the required steps with an acceptable, if not outstanding ratio of knowledge to ignorance.

Throughout, I glanced at my watch hoping against hope that the time would flee, making rounds end early; my one hope was reduced to the game clock running out. This was not to be. I entered the last room like a condemned man awaiting sentencing. There was no escape. All that remained was too horrible to contemplate as dread choked off my breath. My presentation of the first patient left no doubt that I had an incomplete understanding of her status. In addition to her original diagnosis of congestive heart failure, she had a new problem created by my neglect, over- diuresis with resultant dehydration and renal dysfunction. Nowhere to hide, I answered three questions in a row with, "I don't know." One such answer raises eyebrows, two raise doubts and three a red flag. Dr. Richardson's response was to walk up to me and gently kick me in the shins. It left a mark on my self esteem no less prominent than a slap across the face.

The patient would be fine with medication reduction and fluid intake changes, but the doctor? This was the culmination of four years of class work and clinical rotations; my first taste of responsibility, and I had done no one proud. Rounds mercifully ended with a sidebar between the attending and the supervising resident, no doubt identifying me as the one who needed more supervision. The Assistant Chief then came over and in the gentlemanly manner of Richmond Virginia said, "Let's get a cup of coffee." Seated in a booth, coffee served, I blurted out the plea of the condemned, the mitigation before sentencing. "It's not ignorance, it's fatigue." I told him of never getting to the room. In my memory I do not recall any specific suggestions from the professor but do remember how good it felt to sit and drink coffee and not want to go back. But go back I did. Mercifully for all concerned the house staff changed to a new service one week later.

Relieved and with a resolve to never face that problem again, I went to the next assigned ward the night prior to starting on service. No beeper went off as I read through each chart, interviewed and examined each patient. I got to know them as if they were my own, which they soon would be. I wrote an on service note organizing the information. When Monday came, I knew what had to be done and did it. This habit of *pre-rounding* has stood me in good stead through the years. I did it on weekends on call all through my years in practice, learning my charges on Friday nights before the Saturday deluge began. Deep in my memory resides the lesson that taught the responsibility demanded of those who care for others, delivered at the end of a shoe.

THEY MADE ME SICK

Uncertainty shadowed every step as he assumed the title of first year resident, newly arrived at a prestigious New York medical training program from one lesser known. One week before he had been that Man-Child of a physician, an intern, just assuming professional competence, finally comfortable with the responsibilities that accompanied the M.D on the diploma. It was possible to stay and be a big fish in a familiar small pond where the instructors were known, their expectations ingrained, the code of acceptable behavior adopted. After four years of medical school in addition to internship, he belonged. This was a place that would have provided a comfort zone for residency but instead the choice was to go to the "best" training program that would have him.

He was now the resident, the go-to guy, the one who knows what to do. Those from Harvard or Yale surely did. There was backup available but not at 2 a.m., especially if an acute emergency occurred. He had in anxious moments read of all manner of physiologic disasters in *The Manual of Medical Therapeutics* and joked about learning what to do until the doctor arrived. This was little comfort while bobbing in the sea of insecurity that was the prestigious residency, which a few weeks ago had seemed the most direct route to excellence.

Shortly after arriving rounds were held with the Chief of Medicine, the Nobel Prize winning Chief of Medicine. As if this was not intimidating enough, the medical house staff team rounded with three professors instead of the usual one, to allow teaching expertise in several areas. Teaching rounds consisted of the intern discussing the cases of all new patients admitted to the floor, and then withstanding the barrage of inquiries by the attending trio. The questioning of a supreme court appellate could not have been closer, as each professor probed the house staff presentations for a teachable point or simply to impress the others with his superior knowledge in the game that was roundsmanship.

The newly minted intern's presentation began: "The patient is a forty-five year old diabetic woman of Puerto Rican extraction who is requiring huge doses of insulin and developing rashes at the injection sites." The professor pounced: "Have you tried different types of insulin?" One interrupted. "Yes, we've tried beef and pork insulin..." recited the intern, beginning to fidget. "Have you used steroids which can paradoxically lower sugar in insulin resistant patients?"quizzed a second. "No, we haven't done that yet," said the intern glancing desperately around for support. Before any could be offered the Chief, who could no longer bear his observer status began," I wrote a paper on insulin resistance," he said to the hushed room." It's due to sensitivity to certain large proteins in the insulin which can be overcome by boiling it at....degrees for exactly....minutes." No one willing to controvert the Chief, the Nobel Prize winning Chief, they moved on to other aspects of the patient's care.

That evening, the intern energized by the suggestions asked for the new resident's collaboration in the biochemistry project suggested on rounds. In the small house staff laboratory used mostly for urinalysis, they had set up a beaker of water containing a large thermometer with a Bunsen burner below. The water bubbled as the intern lowered a bottle of regular insulin suspended by surgical thread into the beaker and timed the immersion with the stopwatch component of his graduation gift. At the precise second prescribed he withdrew the vial and cooled it.

As the intern and resident entered her room, the patient, a rotund, taciturn lady reclined comfortably in bed; pictures of her three children, dressed in their finest, adorned the bedside table. After a perfunctory "*buenas noches*," the intern injected a small dose of insulin taken from the precisely boiled bottle into her IV tubing. No more than thirty seconds later she sat bolt upright in bed, eyes wide with fright and said "*Me enfermam!*" "They made me sick," collapsing into an atonal heap. There was no measurable blood pressure and a barely palpable pulse. Sweat oozed from every pore in the room, the healers' matching hers. "This is it," said the resident audible only to himself, with the intern deferring to the point of physically taking a step backward.

"Nurse get a crash cart," the resident heard his voice say. "Epinephrine, 0.3 ccs sub q stat, oxygen, Benadryl, steroids," emerged from the depths of his brain— anything ever known to reverse anaphylaxis, that most extreme of allergic reactions. No better, the patient remained a silent testament to good intentions gone horribly wrong. Boluses of fluid, pressors, more epinephrine. His epitaph was being written as the seconds became minutes: "he couldn't follow simple instructions and wound up killing a patient." A third round of each and she began to stir as pressure in her arteries became sufficient to perfuse her brain. Slowly, pulse stronger, slowly, blood pressure measurable, increasing in millimetric amounts but increasing. Her sweat no longer added to the damp likeness surrounding her on the sheets as her blood pressure eventually, gradually, with excruciating slowness, normalized.

In the time slowing trance that had occurred peri-
odically in moments of great stress, every fiber of his
being was focused on that bed. . When he finally looked
up, the hour hand had somehow moved, marking his
patient's journey from life to near death and back again.

Thirty minutes later and assured that she was back
to "baseline", he and the intern walked together feeling the utter fatigue of the oarsman, having expended
his last ounce of energy before collapsing as the finish
line is crossed. The intern laughed nervously as they left
the room. "Boy am I glad you were here. I've never seen
anaphylaxis before." "Neither have I," said the resident.

WHO WERE YOU?
ON MAKING ROUNDS IN A
NURSING HOME

W ho were you? You lay wizened, shriveled of body and mind, grey of hair and spirit. You lay in an impersonal room that reeks of disinfectant, unable to completely erase the smell of that universal marker of territory, urine. Surely this place is not yours. There are occasional pictures, from an earlier era all, for you wouldn't want to enshrine the image of the present. They show family that long since has reduced visitation to a minimum, arriving only when driven by guilt or demanded by medical necessity. The sounds are the creeks and moans of a shipwreck slowly, gradually undergoing its final disincorporation; less often loud and violent than indicating slow, relentless decay. The present is to be endured until it mercifully becomes a distant memory. You cannot now relate how you got to this state. All of your history resides with others. Even the daily maintenance of bodily needs must be provided, supervised, sometimes imposed. You have arrived at the same distant train station as all the others but certainly your journey was unique.

So I wonder, who were you? Were you a titan of industry? Did underlings curry your favor or quake before your pronouncements? I wonder if you accomplished good, a benevolent leader, caring for his charges in every way possible; or just accomplished, by any means, cold and pragmatic, rationalizing the resultant damage. Were you a loyal follower, performing the mundane tasks that keep the world in balance, daily, faithfully for years unending?

Were you a loving mother, daughter or lover? Strange to think of the elderly as having been young, flirtatious, sexual. But surely you were, for if not who begat those who begat us? Did you extend your gifts to the next generation, helping your children raise theirs, sharing the tasks that can burden a young family and partaking of the resultant pleasures?

Did you live life against the current, a bohemian of your time? Were your rebellions small ones, refusing to make your bed because they become unmade each night? Were they large, banishing offenses with violations of family demands, leaving home against all advice, marrying outside the faith? Were you the good child shaking your head at those less considerate, daily finding time to go to church, tend to duties, care for parents?

Your journey, I suspect began there and not here. Was the path illuminated by opportunity or hope or necessity? Was it undertaken gladly as a life adventure or with the resentment of the uprooted?

So many possible routes to the same destination. You are so much more than what remains. You are the sum of all the roads life has placed before you, all you have touched, done or not done. You are a person of value to be comforted, cared for. You are so much more.

INSULATION

With age is lost
The home's veneer
The wires bereft
Of insulation, exposed

Copper coiled, ready
Purpose undermined
By a sudden shock
Unprovoked, causing pain.

So with the occupant
Nerve sheath and subtlety
Long eroded, expose
Sharp edges below.

No longer disguised
Behind a mask
Of humor, restraint
Or manners woven

To make soft the barbs,
Just beneath.
Opinions once thoughtful,
Habits once gentle,

Now lacerate
Unshielded by the insulation,
Long gone from the home
And the one who grows old there.

THAT'S LIFE

CELEBRATION

As the train heard, before seen
As puffs of smoke in the clear blue
Promise of the sky, announces
Its presence, its creeping presence
To shape, to form of trainness
Time used less with each approaching step.

Celebration approaches ever faster
From the distant horizon
One year ago, a hope, a wish
A thought, becomes in the mid-
Distance, a plan, and more
With nearness, haze turns clear.

As the storm clouds gather
Round the seeds within, so worries
Rise like yeast in the darkness
Mix with sleep, and make rest
A sometime thing and
Waking to tasks at night,

To keep the rains at bay,
Knowing all is not knowable
While visions of gloom
Grow near for surely all
Can't be banished, you try
Through plans on plans on plans

As details build, as the train comes
As the celebration approaches
Ever faster, ever closer
Knowing in a Doppler moment
It will ever slower be receding
In the mirror of time

What of the piece missing? (May it be small),
A thing of humor not worthy of the dread
That lurks within us, to be
Soon banished as the celebration
Crosses the horizon to live
In the history we strive to create.

FRIENDS

I have learned to write the year on each entry for I know now more than ever how quickly the numbers accumulate. My friend Dave shocked me by introducing me as his "friend for fifty years." We met and bonded in our teens when we were still trying to create an identity. Through college three friends became six as we found mates who in turn became friends. Joined by sports and shared college experiences, we grew closer as we created our common history. The bonds grew with marriage, living as an extended family in Richmond and sharing the joys of parenthood. Once when Gabby, our friend's daughter, visited we went through a box of old pictures. I asked her what were the odds of finding a picture of her family. Of course the game was rigged because the answer was 100%. Most vacations and life cycle events were experienced with three families; the family of friends we had created from three unrelated but loving tribes.

We knew each other's past, or as much as anyone can share. We lived each other's present, even from afar. We supported each other when needed. We wept when there was little else we had to offer. But always there was a need to see each other, a force of almost physical dimension. Sharing the vacation was far more important than the destination. Distance existed only in miles but never in feelings. By the first hug we were back. Time had not passed. The shared joy of proximity had not diminished. Separation, it seems, had created a sweeter reunion. The end of each visit was made bearable by the planning for the next.

I'm not sure we are our real selves together, but I have no doubt we are our best selves together. We may not show each other the rough edges that our families or mates might see; but we are there to discuss or console, to laugh together at the absurd, or advise if given permission. And we are there to love. We are there.

I would expect no less from our family of choice.

LOGIC IN THE RAMBLES

There was a gossamer thread of logic linking the ramblings. At 93 and recently moved to a rented house—hers was declared unfit for habitation—the confusion mounted. "Where am I? Am I dead? What is this room? Is this heaven? Is God in every room? Is his name Jehovah?" This showed more organized thought than usual, with the anxiety preserved thanks to the omission of tranquilizers by her aide, who believed the patient ate better when not sedated.

She revealed some knowledge of the past, remembering my name and that of my mother, dead 36 years. She knew her daughters. She knew the name of her departed husband but claimed not to be able to see his picture. She could read my T-shirt and included a word from it in her questions. She knew she was in a wheel chair in a new place.

She helped solve the riddle of which was the missing link, cognition or sensory input. I believe that she demonstrated clearly this was primarily a processing issue.

She did reveal that death was close enough to the surface of consciousness to dominate her thoughts and conversation. She did not appear to fear death as she did fear not knowing what to do; an extension of school time anxiety that led her to vomit each day on the corner as she approached elementary school, unsure if her assignments were performed to a sufficiently high standard.

She revealed a belief in an omnipresent God.

She is approaching the end of her years—a journey which has outlived the joy—and I believe she knows it. Always insecure even when road signs were clear, she now fears most being lost. Indecision haunts her, magnified immeasurably by not knowing what is expected of her, what is her duty—since she met her obligations throughout life with responsibility and caring. What is the modern equivalent of homework? In lieu of vomiting, she has the empty feeling of something missing and no longer having the means of finding it.

So she reveals herself in the details of the delirium. With aides, a rental house, small tablets and ever more painful visits, those who knew her best suffer her present along with her, victims of "good genes." I think we all wish for her a painless and peaceful crossing of the river. Her words tell me she has reached the same conclusion.

A VISIT TO GRANDMA DOTTY

The rented house was neat, well kept and ominous. Trepidation turned to dread as they caught sight of the deep orange pillars found attractive only by Florida developers. The wife let herself in with the key she kept while trying to feel in control—a descriptive so far from reality as to be laughable.

Her mother's caregiver of ten years was in the living room keeping a distant eye on the drooping white head barely extending over the top of the wheelchair. Twenty four hour a day supervision did no more than the *successful* hip operation to salvage a woman who had loved and supported her two daughters in every way possible each day of their lives. Somehow after 94 years of close observation that woman had escaped, hopefully to a better place.

Left was a thin, frail shell housing a lost soul who recognized no one, not even the daughter who sang to her
when nothing else calmed the agitated perseveration,
the incessant repeating of, "I'm dead. Where am I? What
is this place?" It did no good to disagree for this only
heightened the anxiety behind the words. Medication
caused drowsiness and refusal to eat. Pictures or bringing the great grandchildren only added to her confusion as she tried to understand who was disturbing her
routine. In desperation her daughter sat and painted
bright nail polish on Grandma's fingers, which once
stroked her children while praising their every effort.
The manicure was accepted passively.

The visits were endured like incisions lacerating the
soul, as each effort to share love was interpreted as an
intrusion at best and more frequently as an assault. This
play of pathos ended with each participant in tears, the
mother in fear and the daughter in helpless frustration
and loss, softened slightly by the knowledge of the wonderful, generous woman who used to answer to Mama,
but knowing that all would be repeated in one week.

DOTTY'S STORY: ONE WEEK LATER

We get the call, at 1:30 AM. We speak with the Broward sheriff's deputy and say we'll be there. "Not necessary," we are told, but we come because my wife has to. The police are still there writing up endless reports. The caretaker is awake and plans to spend the night. She wanted to be sure the family's wish for no CPR or heroics would be honored. She then called rescue who *pronounced* Dotty and the police who committed her demise to endless reports.

We see Dotty, pale and cold, her mouth agape—In protest? In an effort to garner one more breath? In forming the words "It's okay?"—but soundless, the anxiety spent, the disorientation between this world and the next now redirected to the afterlife, if such exists, or released into the atmosphere if all ends with the final breath.

We sit and talk with the caregiver—one final debriefing, memorizing Dotty's last moments—as we await the hearse. Two men come in suits and 3a.m. ties, the night shift; all efficiency and politeness, they explain as gently as possible the immediate future. Dotty fills more of the stretcher than I thought possible, her contracted body extended by the plastic wrap and covered in red velvet shaped to match the stretcher and block any hint of who lies beneath.

They leave just before 4a.m. as do we. One policeman is still doing reports in his car as we pull away.

The next day is replete with calls to the funeral home, endless intra-family communications to see if the closest can agree on a date for the funeral, review of the paper trail and searching for misplaced documents. The hour-long drive to the funeral home is filled with phone calls to co-ordinate, to inform, to accept condolence. We visit the funeral home and decide on a Sunday funeral, the next day, as least disruptive—a criterion that Dotty would no doubt have approved.

We meet on Saturday at the funeral home and decide on a graveside service at 11:30am. We need to be there 45 minutes early. Calls are made to a scattered family and to friends who are tasked with calling others. Plans are made for two days of shiva, one in Weston after the funeral and one the next evening at our house in Miami. We have left a separate $500 check for a rabbi, if needed, which it is when our local clergy prove unreachable. On the drive back to Weston from the funeral home, the two daughters are called by the rabbi and introduce him to the mother of their formative years, sharing stories and smiles.

No one sleeps well Saturday night. The morning of the funeral we awaken before the sun and are at the cemetery thirty minutes earlier than required. We sit in a small, spare room around an oval table and discuss procedure with the funeral director. Slowly the room fills with our children and theirs. My son arrives sleepless, having traveled all night.

Each of us, my wife especially, is joyful at the realization that this room is filled with the life's accomplishment of her parents; it is full of beauty, energy and life. Friends fill the hall as the rabbi comes in and asks the grandchildren for their memories of Grandma Dorothy. The stories are as unique as life itself, filled with laughter and tears.

The two daughters and their husbands have a front row seat at the graveside. The thought that we are next occurs to more than one of us. The rabbi speaks well and then the family, with poems and stories and feelings, reminding those present of the good memories and gifts of wisdom that will live on. We form a line to help bury Grandma with dirt held by tradition on the reverse side of the shovel—why I am still not sure.

Monday night is a Shiva at our house. Our cantor is there, contrite after missing our earlier messages because she was out of town. We are concerned that we might have only eight attendees, insufficient for a minion. There are 47. We try to figure out which way is east, then the cantor and a second soloist conduct a beautiful service. Friends work early and late to set up, clean, then unwrap food for late comers.

The next week sweeps by, each day filled with exhaustion and sisterly cooperation as they sort through stacks of memories: poems written by Grandma to our children on their bar and bat mitzvahs, photos of happy times, notes from Dotty's mother.

By Tuesday, each trip back means a Prius full of artifacts in plastic containers stuffed to the brim with picture frames, a small metal cable car music box playing "I Left My Heart in San Francisco", delicate tea cups, a gold plated clock in a plastic enclosure. Each drawer is a treasure trove and a challenge—what to keep, what to offer to the children, what to donate. After endless sorting of jewelry, trying to decide if it is real or costume, they find a list of each piece and its composition.

While they sort, I go through the internet to find someone to pick up all the unwanted items from the large: couches, kitchen and dining room tables, to the small: the bedside hospital tray, the lamps, the artificial orchid in fake water that was last year's Mother's Day present. Most, like the Salvation Army and Habitat for Humanity make it clear that anything scratched or stained will not be taken, and they cannot come until after the 15th—the date we must leave the apartment. We eventually book College Hunks who haul everything to Good Will; the un-salable to be recycled, the rest sold. The two college kids come to give us an estimate: about $600 for an entire seven by twelve foot, open topped truck. I ask what they got in geometry, and they prove their Pythagorean skills by filling every millimeter with un-salables. The two cheerful body builders from a gay rights group, 'Out of the closet' pick up the rest a couple of days later, with not a word about the broken chair or the leg that falls off the table as they lift it.

A few pieces go to family. We will take the three TVs for our new North Carolina home. No one else has room or desire for rest. Smaller knick-knacks will be given to the kids at a later date.

Our mourning is characterized by relief and resurrecting memories of a person long departed and long suffering, now relieved of the burdens of residual life; and by cooperation of two daughters that would have made Dotty proud. The memories are sweet and need to be shared with those who came too recently to know. The recollection, the sharing, the relief, the release, this is what fills our days and leaves us in a really good place one week later.

APHORISMS TO LIVE BY SUGGESTED BY FAMILY AND FRIENDS ...AND ME

A successful parent raises a child who can pay for his (her) own psychotherapy.*

Kids come in different speeds.*

All disease is sudden. One day you consider yourself well and then a label is placed.

When you are well, you never think you will be sick and when you are sick, you think you will never be well. Both are false most of the time.

No one is ever perfectly happy with their appearance. So don't spend an inordinate amount of time dwelling on perceived imperfections.

It's (usually) comforting to be able to blame your illness on your parents. (Also true for your longings, unfulfilled state, neuroses etc).

Take responsibility for all areas of your life, except your illnesses and longings and neuroses. See above.

Less is more. This could be the cure for all the excesses to which we are subjected by the world or by ourselves.

Corollary: **Moderation in all things.**

In life you gotta show up. In relationships and especially in childrearing, phoning it in just won't do. Promises and excuses are a band-aid hiding the wound from your eyes but not healing it.*

Life is a Pop Quiz* or as Forrest Gump said: **Life is like a box of chocolates: you never know what you are going to get,** or for that matter what challenges awaits you. Don't shrivel up worrying about it, just know that something new is around the corner, good or bad; that's life, accept it.

---

* Courtesy of Dr. Henry Storper

Take 2 and bunt.   Baseball aphorisms rarely have a universal meaning.

There's no 'I' in team.   Nor is there an eye or an aye or for that matter an Aye For an Eye. I told you baseball aphorisms were just invented to keep kids busy so they wouldn't chew tobacco.

I've set enough examples.   Grandma Dotty at age 65.

When all else fails, lower your standards. (My personal favorite, by nephew Sam Gustman at age 15)

WYSIWYG What you see is what you get.

OLD FRIENDS

Old friends, in town, before a cruise takes them
To the endless floating buffet on the way
To private islands and cookouts on the beach.

We meet over dinner and catch up
In the old friends way.
Talk of family, now grandchildren more than kids.

Talk of how we cobble together a day,
What is our new work, their new home,
Jobs some cling to, for how long, and why.

We talk of illness, sometimes before
Other guests arrive, so things intimate
Can be kept with those who really care.

Though all others know, for they are near,
Aware of scans, and offer
To drive, to be there for support.

Was the talk really so different
Back then? Were we? Do we morph
Like butterflies as seasons pass?

We who complained still do.
The optimists still are, knowing life offers
Sweet fruit, or soon to be.

Those who create works of art:
Even better in weeks of leisure
Instead of days, stolen from work and family.

We recall places we've been, they've been,
Places we will go soon, God willing
And the market stays high.

The story of our kids, middle aged!
Stable in job and family, except
For the cruel illness that sometimes stalks.

The grandkids provide the joy, the smiles.
Praised for growth, or a clever word
Or anything graded A+, or different,

Or caring, or sweet,
Or said in passing
On the phone with grandma.

Old friends come from far,
Far enough to make it a trip,
Too far between visits,

As life flows by our window
And we recall the stops along the way
We have shared together.

THE CRASH

The crash is coming as I watch in slow motion; it progresses, a ballet disastre unfolding so slowly it can be understood and anticipated, not with fear but through the eyes of the dispassionate, the marvel of being at once the observer and the observed. As I sit at the end of a long line of cars waiting for the rush hour red to become green, it comes. Lights from the distance are felt as much as viewed in the mirror. Something seems wrong as it approaches at rates unsustainable in the choked arteries of the early evening rush hour. In that blink of recognition time slows. Each second is experienced as a minute or several, allowing observation, analysis, and anticipation but strangely not fear. As the lights approach, the first thought is: this car is not going to stop.

The only decision lies with the other driver, for there is no where I can go. The lights slowly grow as my world view concentrates upon the rectangle of glass that is my rear view mirror. I am aware of the meaning of enlarging light circles. Finally my mirror is filled not with circles but a wall of light, strangely followed by darkness as the headlights of my approaching nemesis dip below the point of reflection. I now hear, not yet feel but clearly hear, the slow crunch not unlike an empty beer can being gradually compressed. The sound begins in the distance and I am aware that it is coming closer, gaining on my inert presence. I grip the wheel tighter a reflex unaccompanied by emotion, only acceptance of the inevitable, the unavoidable. Then the physical is restored as the pace of time quickens. I am suddenly thrust forward with such force that my glasses fly off my face and onto the dashboard. My compressed enclosure is pushed to the right onto the sidewalk and I am struck again. Loudness returns, as does the sensation of having each joint stressed, the result of parts of me surging and stopping independently. Finally quiet returns as I watch myself get out of the car and the word 'accident' forms in my scrambled brain.

The newly licensed teen cries as she realizes the consequence of looking down at her beeping device while maintaining 40 M.P.H. speed. She is not visibly hurt nor is her pre-teen brother in the seat next to her. She says she never saw me, never hit the brake until after impact when she hit the gas pedal by mistake and struck me again. I struggle to make sense of events, hand my cell phone to the frightened girl, tell her to call her parents and begin with "We're both okay but—" I call the police but don't know my location, just recite the name of the church across the street. I must have called my son who in my post concussive malcognition becomes the parent. I hear the words of the policeman as if he were speaking an unfamiliar tongue.

The contents of my trunk now litter the street opposite the church whose name I can't recall. The trunk of my car now resides in the back seat. The brain that minutes before dissected each microsecond now can't remember my address. Over several days my brain returns to baseline but with the indelible imprint of the moments when time shifted gears.

Is this an instinct imbedded long ago in our developing brains, all senses hyper-alert at moments of primal danger? I have read of such altered perceptions occurring in combat or the modern equivalent, contact sports. Have we learned to suppress it as our cortex grew? Could it be that this altered state of perception is so stressful that thought processes are slowed thereafter until the chemical soup that is *thought*, is reconstituted? If it takes threat of such magnitude to arouse this preservation hyper-state, though fascinating and unforgettable, I would prefer it rests undisturbed in the deepest recesses of my paleo being.

WE SHOULD TELL OUR CHILDREN

All three couples recalled the close calls that chilled in the retelling. We have had similar conversations with other couples as soon as a certain comfort level is reached, where honesty trumps the fear of exposure as a "bad parent." We recounted those situations that visit a father or mother in their worst nightmares: having a child wander off, nearly drown, or escape a horrendous fate by sheer luck. Good parenting should anticipate such situations and avoid the danger altogether. *Should*, a word so authoritarian and idealistic, yet so flawed in reality. Who can watch a child every second of every day? How would a parent know when the dinner is cooked, the laundry done, not to mention the world of diversion such as reading, TV, daydreaming, or the ultimate dereliction of duty, a nap?

We'd all done it, every single one, red-faced in the re-telling: the frantic search around the house, at the beach, at the airport. "I just looked away for a second!" Our kids turned up—Thank you God—and we lived with the guilt and swore it would never happen again, but it did at a different time and place, but it did. The dangers grew along with the child's age, mobility and willpower or occasionally willful disobedience. "Don't move from here," and he does, or a famous quote in our family from a three year old mumbling to himself after being given a directive, "Maybe I will and maybe I won't." Where is the chapter in the parenting handbook on anticipating that attitude and resultant situations? Surely with growth comes increased autonomy, not always accompanied by increased common sense.

Then there are the teenaged years and the associated feelings of invincibility. We all tried to control the uncontrollable. Who can anticipate each late night decision? Have we all been so beaten down and aware of our dwindling influence by this point that half measures are the best we can do? "Be home by 11 p.m., no more than one friend in the car with you, call me if for any reason you can't drive and I'll get you, no questions asked," all signs of how powerless we are in the struggle to limit teenaged risk taking.

We chose to share these near disasters with our children many years ago. They are now parents themselves who must trust us with the safety of their children. Have we diminished our credibility as caretakers by sharing our misadventures? Have we de-stigmatized mistakes, making them an acceptable part of parenting when we fessed up? I would argue for full disclosure. The next generation of parents needs to know what lies in wait. Maybe our experiences will help them avoid even one of our pitfalls. Maybe they will be better parents than we have been. Isn't that what we have always wanted, for each generation to be an improvement on the last? At the very least they will learn that complete control is as impossible for a parent as is the notion of providing a risk free environment. When a scary event occurs they are not automatically self-branded as incompetent, "bad" fathers and mothers; they are imperfect guardians just like the rest of us. They too will have tales of come-close events that will rock their foundations, but must be shared with the next generation of parents.

RETIREMENT

RETIREMENT ADVICE

Dave said I deserved to enjoy myself.
Monty said I'd wind up driving the grandchildren to school every day.

Sheila said I'd travel to exotic places.

Ilene said Wheeeeeeeeeeeee.

Alan said to be sure my money wouldn't run out.

Henry said great, but he'd be too anxious to do it.

Woody said keep busy.

Don said always have a back door.

Schwab said invest early.

A patient said try many things and give yourself permission to change.

Marilyn said me too.

Many said they were happy for me and then looked inward.

Dave also said I'd do less and it was okay.

Most have been right, more or less, and helpful. The lack of negativity was comforting. My hunt did not turn up an 800 pound gorilla whose existence I was denying. It did show that most of my peers were dealing with retirement at the intellectual level, coming to varying conclusions, some feeling anxiety. When they get to the point of emotional acceptance, when peace arrives, they will know it's time.

RETIREMENT DAY +1

I saw my last patient yesterday at 1 p.m. The day was not what I imagined. There was no party, no fire-works, no jugglers. But it was sweet nonetheless. It was Christmas and then some. Like the prior week patients brought wine, flowers, small wooden handcrafts from their native countries and, of course, homemade mango jam. Many came without a medical reason just to say goodbye. The last was best of all. The daughter and wife of a very difficult but likeable man came to thank me. He had problems both medical and behavioral. Though he had died more than a year ago, they wanted to be sure I knew how grateful they were. "You need to hear this," they began. "This office was a safe place my dad would go when anything was wrong. He would be listened to. He trusted your advice." They came with a bottle of champagne for me and sweets for the office staff. The visit ended with a group hug. It was far better than a party and was my own personal fireworks display.

It was like Christmas not just because of the presents. People were lighter, less focused on problems. They were in these days, friends more than patients. Their thick charts documented the decades many had come. They came to focus on me. What was my plan? Was I well? Was I staying or moving? And they came to wish me well—a living wake with things said in parting that "need to be said," leaving everyone richer.

Like all of life we focus on the problems that arise. We infrequently show real gratitude or even affection for those we interact with every day. Do we not have permission to share these feelings without crossing some societal boundary? Of course there was a brief *thanks* or 'I'll let you know how this works.' Maybe my patients did express these things and I was not ready to hear them until now. Maybe I was the one who was too focused to really listen. And maybe now in my last days in the office, I needed the reassurance that my thirty-eight years of practice had meaning to others. This was a going away present far better than any I had envisioned. A cake emblazoned with many candles. How sweet.

They said, "You need to hear this."

And I did.

THE POWER OF AGING

I'm taking one of those free online courses in micro-economics. Strange choice? In typical rabbinic fashion I answer a question with a question, "Why not?" With all those four hour biology and chemistry labs there wasn't much room for the liberal arts, even those like psychology and economics—which in different ways help explain human motivations and responses. It is easy to attend, relatively stress free, and a great alternative to the endless Law and Order marathons on TV. Since I have chosen not to take the course for credit I can take the quiz or move on to the next set of lectures, dwelling on those that enlighten areas of mental murkiness or seem relevant to today's headlines.

Therein resides the power, the inherent strength of "take it or leave it" that goes with retirement. The first hint of what lies ahead was the "short timer syndrome." In the last few months of working I realized that "have to" became "if I choose to" as in: must I complete forty continuing medical education credits to renew my license? To quote my grandson, three years old at the time, "maybe I will and maybe I won't." Eventually I did choose to take the CME courses but for reasons of choice, not obligation.

Actually my first introduction to this concept was thirty years ago from my mother-in-law, then sixty-five years old and deciding not to celebrate a religious holiday. "What about the example you're setting?" we asked with tongue in cheek. "I've set examples my whole life and now it's up to you."

So we come to the essence of this issue, power, the power of decision making. Is it driven by economics, obligation to family or group, or has the power migrated to the senior not unlike the gray hair that leaves the scalp and winds up in our ears? Will I trim them or not?

Maybe I will.

And maybe I won't.

EXTRA TIME

The World Cup carries with it a special lexicon, especially the concept of *extra time*. After an exhausting ninety minutes of running, should the score be tied, the players get an extra thirty minutes to decide the outcome, to continue pursuing the victory that has so far been elusive. They are essentially given a *do-over*, an extra third of their game.

How wonderful if we could all, at the end of our allotted time, have a little more to finish up the unfinished, make whole that which is in formation. But who actually *finishes* their life's tasks in the time allowed? Is there not another life cycle event just one calendar flip away? How will our seeds flower? As long as extra time is not a vessel for overwhelming burdens, most would say, "Bring it on."

Many of us, people of a "certain age", are in fact experiencing *extra time* right now. We no longer spend most of our days working. With retirement we are given a blank calendar to fill, limited only by our imaginations, savings and physical abilities. My sister grows vast flower gardens and leaves her watch behind as she waters, or repots, or plants. Her switch from grant writing was instantaneous and oh so welcome. At our last medical school reunion, one classmate told of studying economics after retirement and teaching personal finance courses to high school students. Another told of always loving auto racing and how he bought a race car to endlessly modify and even race. Others have become guardians-ad-litem, standing up for neglected children.

Our family obligations are mostly met, our grown children having gifted the sweetest dividend of all, grandchildren. Some friends have elected to donate their parenting skills to the next generations out of need, a love of parenting, or both. We can now show up at every school show, ceremony, or game. We no longer participate in the tug of war for our time in which work often prevailed.

The *extra time* is a gift. I don't feel a compulsion to use every minute in a productive fashion; but I do want to enjoy as much of it as possible. Unlike the World Cup players, I do not know how much *extra time* has been granted and perhaps that is a good thing, for it allows room for hope—hope to continue *extra time* for as long as it is still appealing. So I view this period, as do the World Cup players, as a time to achieve ends, to see how the game turns out, and to avoid if possible the penalty kicks that life and sport may deliver.

SOCIAL INSECURITY

The letter said my Medicare costs were going up despite the fact that my income had plunged, as often happens when one retires. I could make an appointment but the first one was more than a month away and wouldn't correct the record until after the New Year, which was not acceptable for reasons still unclear to me. 1-800-Medicare said to call Social Security, and I did. Walk in they suggested. No problem. Do it soon and start the New Year right.

And so at 9:20 a.m. I strolled into the Social Security office on SW 211 Street under the expert direction of Google Maps. Untold, however, was the lack of identifying signage facing the street and the absence of parking spaces. The only sign suggested on-street parking which was nonexistent. I decided to visit the parking lot of a Humana clinic down the block.

Upon entering the low, cement block building it seemed more suited for a hurricane shelter than a regional Social Security office handling intake of retirees, the disabled, the over-billed. The main entrance faced an alley and did have a large sign—invisible from the street—announcing the building's function. Not five feet inside was a metal detector manned by two very serious, pistol carrying security officers. My pockets were emptied a la TSA screening and my jacket was patted down sufficiently to discover the emergency English Breakfast tea bags, which were assessed for threat and found wanting, as I was passed through. The need for metal detectors became clear as I listened to the often frustrated and demanding public plead their cases in the semi-exposed windows defining one wall of the waiting room. The employees sat behind thick protective-appearing glass windows with a speaking hole situated above the forehead of the seated applicant and a small crack for air at the bottom. I'm guessing the glass could withstand mortar rounds.

At 9:21 a.m. I cleared security and broke one of their basic rules. I asked a security guard a question: "What do I do now?" The overworked guard whispered, "Go to the machine in the back room and register." I guess he didn't want it publically known he was a softy and would then be deluged by help requests. There were two large waiting rooms each with about fifty chairs and standing room around the periphery. I located the kiosk, which worked more easily than the airline variety. I chose a language, entered my social security number, pressed four for *other* when asked for a general category of why I came today and it spit out a lotto-like ticket number A-286. At least I was at the beginning of the alphabet. Those poor suckers with Z at the start might just as well pitch a tent. I sat in the rear waiting room and barely heard numbers being called. Moving to waiting area A, I realized that the fifty black plastic chairs were only about three-quarters full. I took one near the front and found them comfortable and adequately spaced. To my amazement A-271 was called followed by A 272! What an efficient system. Where are those Tea Party doubters who scoff at government efficiencies? In less than five minutes my number was called. I walked into the private area adjacent to waiting room A and went to my window, one of thirty. A smiling, thin, middle-aged lady greeted me pleasantly and asked why I was there. I told her it had to do with increased charges for Medicare parts B and D. The letter Medicare sent said that I should con-tact them for any of several reasons, one of which was a change in employment status. Since retiring from medi-cal practice in September 2012 and administration in May 2013, I qualified. So did Marilyn, who quit in June, 2012. The affable lady typed a couple of lines then said,

"Have a seat and they'll call you by name. We're just screening problems now. It speeds things up." "How do you know my name?" I asked. "You entered your Social Security number." Duh. "Do many people you encounter get angry?" I ask, thinking again of the metal detectors and the thick glass. She says, "No, maybe I diffuse it with a smile." I forget to ask her estimate of my waiting time. Just as well.

I gloomily traipse back to the bull pen and take a seat in the first row. A man in the row behind is relating in a mild Jamaican accent: "Someone accessed all my information and got my check." This makes my issue seem insignificant. Names are called along with numbers, some in Spanish, some in English. How do they know? I remember question one at the kiosk, language preference. These people forget nothing. Bored already, I make a chart of the frequency of Spanish vs. English instructions, which turns out to be nearly equal. Slightly less often is the "last call" list, those who have walked out. Not a good sign.

9:40a.m.—A well tanned Latin lady with earrings four inches high saying "Trust No Bitch" stomps away rapidly from a nearby window, not pleased. There is a large monitor up front which flashes messages in rapid rotation. It is currently urging me to go on line to Social Securtiy.gov. Honestly I would if I could. Who wouldn't? Adjacent signs tell us to silence cell phones and take no photos. There goes my idea for a photo booth to memorialize this experience in an 8x10 glossy. I notice that I have left my cell phone in the car. For the first time of many today the "leave vs. possibly losing my turn" conundrum is considered and rejected. I don't want to join the "last call" brigade, even more than I want my phone and the iced tea waiting half a block away.

Screen: A cat walks across a computer key board to show how easy it is to retire; even a cat can do it! The pussycat pension program!!! Could they be more insulting? The next message informing that translators are available in Spanish, Chinese, what looks like Greek or Russian alphabet and Polski. It next tells of a "Direct Express debit card." For medical expenses? It doesn't say.

9:57a.m.—Really loud voices calling numbers and names grate more and more.

Screen: Urges us to Please keep children in reception area supervised at all times. This is adjacent to a sign prohibiting food, drink, smoking and fun. (Just kidding about the "fun" but it is understood). I guess parents are supposed to supervise kids using video games or just yelling at them.

10a.m. The "Trust No Bitch" earring lady (known hereafter as the earring lady) rushes back in and says loudly to clerk at window #13 "You skipped my number." To her credit, clerk 13 (why don't they just wear sports jerseys with their numbers front and back) de-escalates the encounter and calmly replies, "I called it three times." Large woman noteworthy for huge butterfly tattoo covering right lower arm, already sitting at that window chimes in unhelpfully, "I heard her call you." Tension mounts as earring lady decides on her next move. It is to storm away and out the metal detector. (? To get a bazooka?) I gather my papers and inch away from window 13, gratefully noticing the sign, "Firearms and Weapons Prohibited."

10:07a.m. I risk a visit to the men's room. I stand and find that both feet are numb—from prolonged sitting on inflexible plastic chairs—and limp forward while holding on lest I fall and am carried to the disabled line in room B and lose my real place in room A. The men's room is surprisingly, amazingly spotless. It is a one-seater in an office with more than fifty men. Was it to undergo an imminent inspection? The sink provides water, the soap dispenser squirts gooey liquid into my hand and the toilet flushes. Take that you Tea Party doubters of government efficiency. If the House of Representatives ran as smoothly as the water in this federal facility..... Well you get the idea. I dry my hands in the loud-speaker- stifling-electric-dryer, straining to hear if my name is being called by some sadistic clerk who notes everyone entering the loo. Nothing even vaguely sounding like my name, as I exit and return to my seat magically cured of my limp; wondering if the onlookers think of me as a faker who has forgotten his malady.

Earring lady strolls by all smiles and conciliation as she waits for #13 and says, "It's not you. It's the board." Clerk-13 says quietly but firmly, "I called." Earring Lady (to be known hereafter as EL if she ever comes back) answers, "I guess I missed it." She sits as I feel safer in moving back to my seat near window 13. Three minutes later she stands with a smile and says, "Have a happy holiday." Baltimore would be proud.

With few alternatives I watch security, now numbering three, each visibly armed. They identify a crisis in the making, the merging of the lines for metal detection and those registering for numbers. With command presence they separate both groups, create order out of entropy. Two straight lines and a no man's land between are created, restoring order.

Screen: as if on cue: "It is a Federal offense to threaten or harm a U.S. government employee in performance of their duties." Maybe earrings was motivated by this missive. Another triumph for government's ability to communicate with its citizens.   The screen now presents helpful tips about avoiding identity theft. Nowhere is "Don't shop at Target" mentioned. Another reminder about needing an interpreter in languages that I now realize includes Tagalog. If I were a Tagalog-a-phile how would I read this notice? Perhaps this is one reason why most applicants are in pairs. The afflicted and the I'll-fix-it. Some of the afflicted are clearly identifiable by being in wheelchairs. Some walk slowly, have expressionless faces and are led by the arm. Some have the swollen ruddy complexion suggesting a familiarity with the Budweiser label.

10:16a.m.—A couple in my row leaves amid discord. She wants to stay. He ends the discussion with "Vamos," clearly the final word. She leaves with reluctant foot dragging.

Screen asks: "Did your employer send you here because of E-Verify?" Not having an employer and not knowing what E-Verify is and searching desperately for diversion I reach for my source of all the world's information, Google Mobile on my cell pho.....oops. I'm on a desert island, stranded without food or water and now no access to Google. This treatment must violate the Geneva Convention. I softly break into" Nobody knows, the trouble I seeeeee." My lament is cut short as I begin to attract the attention of the guards, ever alert for a beneficiary about to go over the edge.

10:20a.m.—One hour invested. Beginning the second hour (it sure feels like more than 60 minutes). I notice that very few names are being called, just numbers of the initial triage encounter. I wonder about the organization of office procedures and how to improve them. Other than a snack bar, better parking and thirty more windows I come up empty.

Screen: Know about Social Security. Like us on Facebook! At this point I don't even like them in person.

10:22 a.m.—I first notice a poster with Mr. Sulu in full Star Trek uniform with the earth and stars in the background. In prominent letters, "Oh my, that was easy" and below, "Boldly go to Social Security.gov." If the armed guards weren't so close and I had remembered my phaser I'd send him 'where no man has gone before'.

Screen: Sensing an imminent melt down, the screen happily reports that there will be a 1.5% cost of living increase in January. Unspoken is, "Cheer up gloomy Gus."

A thin black woman/girl in her late teens, dressed in a heavy hooded sweater with a knitted cap (it is a comfortable mid-70s) accompanies an overweight lady in her 40s and does all the talking. The younger woman has all the answers and numbers requested. In five minutes they move on seeming satisfied.

10:27a.m.—Names are called again. At the window, a white guy—age could be anywhere late 40s to 60s—says loudly, "I've had it since I was five years old." From the context of other shouted comments he is referring to social security payments and not hearing loss. He then lists every date he called. His helper: wife? sister? Provides information and the encounter is quick.

Screen: 98% of social security payments are direct deposit. (By this time I am sensing a need for a deposit of my own.) Then obviously reading my mood it flashes "Thank you for your patience." I'm thinking this means thanks for not organizing a revolution, overwhelming the guards and sacking the entire operation—thoughts that I admit have been considered.

I know I am losing patience despite the screen message when I begin to be annoyed by a caregiver fanning herself, the breeze blowing on me. I move over one seat as "Arthur P...., last call to window 6" blasts over the loud speaker.

10:41a.m.—Getting more grumpy and I am about to ask the lady to stop fanning. She must have sensed something because she immediately stops.

10:43a.m.—Seriously considering leaving. I have an appointment for January 21st, five weeks from now. It will surely be quicker then. But, says the angel on the other shoulder, you have already invested almost an hour and a half; you don't know how long the wait will be even with an appointment. Then the first shoulder answers: "Hey fool, have you ever heard of throwing good money after bad." And so adrift in a sea of indecision, I remain.

I notice that everyone is smiling on the screen and on the posters even when discussing such hilarious subjects as getting your benefits verification letter on line. Is Prozac in the water system here?

Not everyone sits passively and awaits their turn. Between calling a name for a specific window and the person showing up, there is an opportunity for information gathering—frequently taken by the less patient—to approximate waiting times or to plead to be taken early because their story is so compelling.

10:55a.m.—I go to the window. I am asking only for a blank piece of paper. "By the way, what is the expected

wait time?" I ask. "Thirty six minutes," she answers without hesitation. But I've been here an hour and twenty I
add informationally. I later learn she means thirty-six
minutes wait for the screening visit. She looks my name
up in the computer and says there were six others before
me, all of whom had no appointments, like me, and all
of whom would have to be fit in (said in scolding voice).
Revised waiting time is three hours. Why I try to explain to her about the letter saying I should come in by
January 1 and the first appointment being January 21,
I do not know. The tone changes as she becomes more
defensive. "You've had that letter a long time." (In the
world of Social Security, three weeks does not seem to
be a long time.) "You shouldn't make an appointment
for such a simple issue as plan costs," she goes on. I could
sense escalation being moments away. The point of my
interloping is not to provoke an argument. I thank her
for the paper, hold up one palm in the universal symbol
of surrender and sit down. I wonder if she has cancelled
my Jan. 21st appointment. Now I can't leave.

Screen: The messages began recycling. It was 11
a.m. suggesting a recycling time of one hour and forty
minutes. Was this correlated with the average waiting
time? Did those clever people know that I would soon be
called? Do waiting times apply to those *fit in*? So many
unknowns. I try to reduce waiting times to a mathemati-
cal equation: X+Y+2 hours * (number of people in the
room)/ clerks who gave a damn- length of time I could

hold out without pulling out my remaining hair and exiting through the nearest window.

11:07a.m.—The girl in the winter outfit is back, waits politely for a client to finish then explains her new information or problem and calmly exits after a minute or two. I get the feeling this ain't her first rodeo.

11:09 a.m.—Three thoughts occur in rapid succession as I scratch my chin. 1. Waiting is getting harder as hunger and lack of a time certain when my incarceration will end combine to dominate consciousness. 2. The Tea Party's call for smaller government is sounding less harsh by the minute. 3. I think my chin whiskers have grown since I arrived.

11:10a.m.—Window 13 closes. Could it be lunch time already? Does this foretell a further slow- down of processing?

11:11a.m.—I review the potential savings, then calculate it as an hourly wage. Where else could I earn hundreds of dollars an hour? I'm still not totally convinced it's worth it. Sitting and waiting violates so many principles established over a lifetime of piecework, which a friend once explained is the economic basis of a private medical practice.

11:19a.m.—The blame game begins. Why am I waiting so long? It's because there are six others without appointments before me, because I came after nine, because Marilyn was late in getting started and didn't tell me she wasn't coming until it was too late. Aha, a scapegoat. It's all her fault. It's—and in she walks, red faced from frustration at going to the wrong building. Seems those pesky social security web sites aren't updated as often as necessary and still contain the old address. All is forgiven. We are in the trenches together. With backup on site I feel I can walk to the bathroom without fear of missing my turn.

11:25a.m.—Part way down the hall I hear my name called. All urges to use the restroom disappear. Marilyn has already gathered up all our papers and we go to window nine together. Mrs. Rojas, a lovely forty something lady greets us and asks for ID—at least that is what I think she requested since the round communication hole is level with my hairline and I'm listening through her protective barrier. I stretch and ask for frequent repeats of key phrases. We swear on threat of perjury that the information we give is true. (Or that my insurance card is blue, I'm not quite sure). I understand the need for this since no documentation of my previous year's income will be available until I file tax returns next April. The fact that that Uncle Sam will take me at my word, even if jail time is possible for prevaricators, is a pleasant surprise. She will need a copy of said tax return brought to this office—BROUGHT?! As in: wait another gazillion hours outside?—"Well you could mail it," she says and hands me an envelope which I use to fan myself back to consciousness. *Att. IRMA* is written at the bottom of the envelope. She is not an employee or even a she, but an acronym for Income Related Monthly Adjustment. "Ha, ha," as we share a hearty chuckle at what passes for humor in the world of the federal bureaucracy.

I am flooded with joy and relief having finished our business in less than ten minutes, including her copying letters proving the dates of our retirement. Now we are the ones wishing her a Merry Christmas and all good things in the New Year. My feet and mood are light as I float past the metal detector. The system works. Government serves a purpose. I'm a Democrat again.

INNER CIRCLE

Acceptance was all I craved, not adulation or even nodding admiration. From the seat in the outer ring of chairs in the Olli (Osher Lifelong Learning Institute) Investments class, I had listened and observed, on the fringes in every way. I was retired, still having the status of a former profession, but being a nubie when it came to the stock market and finance. The inner circle consisted of retired brokers, accountants, a former head of the university's business school, the whole intimidating array.

Sitting for months, I learned the vocabulary, for that is the essence of accounting, a collection of specialized words whose definitions provided the tools for dissecting a company's financial health. Once I had been bold enough to ask if a balance sheet included cash under fixed investments, which was loudly corrected by many voices at once. That exposure of my ignorance of the basics, led to further months of silence.

A new school year meant new members in the group, some of whom had by dint of prior knowledge, job experience or computer skills been admitted to the inner circle, that ring of sixteen chairs that bordered a series of tables rafted together to create the platform for discussion. The former Fidelity executive, the group's leader, sat in a chair that defined the head of the table. The outer row was for the uninitiated, the late arrivers, those who might not stay. There I sat.

With the arrival of new members came new approaches. We would formulate our investment strategy based on sectors of the economy and re-evaluate our make-believe portfolio to see how it conformed to recommended sector allocations. We then created a list of twenty-two variables upon which to judge the value of a stock. Using this list, volunteers would research each stock we "owned" and see how it measured up to a comparable stock and to the sector as a whole. Four volunteers were requested to study one stock or mutual fund each. My hand went up, my wet, slightly trembling hand. I took a single stock, Schlumberger, thinking this would be more straight forward than analyzing a mutual fund, which is basically a company made up of stock holdings of many other companies.

I dove into the task by using the research function of my broker, Charles Schwab. I used an Excel spread sheet to list the twenty-two parameters on the Y axis and Schlumberger and its main competitor on the X axis. After filling in the boxes for current price, P/E ratio and Market Cap, I realized that I did not understand fully the definition of many of the terms, nor their implications. I set aside the first spread sheet and created a second, a dictionary of the financial terms we were using, with definitions provided by Investopedia, a finance educational web site. I was surprised to see that some of the terms were not listed in Investopedia, Wikipedia or any other 'pedia' known to Google.

I then filled in most of the boxes, defining the financial health of the oil drilling support behemoth, Schlumberger. By the time the research was completed, including comparative data for a similar company, sixteen hours of work had been invested, spread over four days. All pertinent data could be reduced to one double sided page, which I brought with me the following Monday.

I volunteered to go first on the pretext that my set of definitions would frame the discussions that followed. In reality, leading off also meant less time for anxiety and fewer comparison papers which might diminish my efforts. I plunged in with an overview of the company, then the definitions, which no one challenged and finally a detailed review of the financial data. There were disclaimers offered that would help gloss over some internal inconsistencies since some of the data was based on the previous calendar year and some on the most recent twelve months. All went well, with some discussion of the implications of obscure terms like "PEG%", a tool for seeing if a stock is appropriately priced. My humility was restored when I gave an incorrect definition for gross revenue. Most classmates seemed satisfied with the presentation and one even said, "Good job." I exhaled, feeling relief and gratitude for the absence of humiliation. I was even surprised that many members of my group had discernible gaps in their knowledge and were grateful for the definitions listed.

The next week I arrived late, delayed by traffic and tasks at home. I sat in one of the outer ring seats. Three members turned at once and waved me to the remaining seat in the inner ring. Only the sounding of trumpets was missing. It took work to get in and would take work to stay in, but I now had a seat at the table.

NO LONGER A DOCTOR

I n the seventh month of retirement I search unsuccessfully for a label. Since 1969 I identified myself as
a doctor. The strength of that association has faded as
the color from a photograph left in the sunlight. There
is still a vague outline, but details are bleached from
my memory. When you don't perform a task daily, along
with the loss of *muscle memory* is the loss of the feeling of
doing the task, of the worry, of the warm reinforcement
when you get it right and really make a difference, of
being that person.

In my seventh month of retirement I still possess a
license to practice. I could open an office tomorrow,
God forbid. I can still reorder a medication for a family
member, or offer a sidewalk consultation when asked.

What I don't do is take responsibility for the welfare of others. With this change, my burden has been lifted but my identity blurred.

If I no longer feel like a doctor then who am I? Not a former doctor, for I still possess the tools and credentials. Am I identified with the new pursuits I am exploring, a college student, a sometime writer, blogger, poet (under the most forgiving designation), a wannabe? This of course raises the issue, *are we what we do?* Our jobs are one of the first categorizers upon meeting someone: after a word of greeting, an exchange of names and somewhere in the next few minutes, "What do you do?" This question is not about hobbies but an occupation, a place in the world defined by your function, the entity you work for, your position. The less conventional may mention a craft or avocation—"I do pottery," or "I grow vegetables." The wealthy may identify with charities or the arts. A working man may show pride in his level of accomplishment, "I am a master plumber."

Once you no longer "do", who are you? As I float in the nebulous limbo of nonidentity, I wonder if it matters. The answer occurs to me when I consider the corollary: *Is retirement a status or is it an abdication, a retreat from the field of battle that is life?* If retirement is a non-status, a gossamer state of semi-invisibility, is it a demeaning label? Do we seek substitute titles, even if they are premature and a bit misleading? For the last seven months that comprise my retirement, I have used a pseudo pro-fession-hobby-pursuit identifier instead of, "I used to be a doctor."

Paul Gustman (note absence of 'M.D.'), ***blogger, writ-er, poet-to- be.***

ON BEING A DOCTOR AGAIN

In my ninth month of retirement, while exercising at the gym, the familiar call intoned: "Is there a doctor in the house, an EMT, anyone with medical training?" Retired or not, I clearly fit in one of these categories. I walked over and while identifying myself noticed a young girl sitting on an exercise apparatus, sweating and unresponsive. She was being held up by well intentioned patrons and staff. The medical issues were not complicated. First I had the helpers lay her flat and elevate her feet. Almost immediately she regained consciousness despite a weak pulse, which appeared regular. She said she had a history of low blood pressure, was taking medication for it, and was not diabetic. She has passed out twice in the past, had a normal echocardiogram recently, no nausea, vomiting, or diarrhea to account for dehydration, no bleeding, no chest or abdominal discomfort.

Holding her hand, I reached deep into memory for a differential diagnosis of common causes of syncope. Being away from medicine for so long, the thought process and questions were not crisp and well ordered as they might have been when these problems were frequently encountered in my ICU practice. Fire rescue had been called so I only owned the problem for these few minutes. I spoke with her father who confirmed the syncope history and that this was the first time she was trying exercise since being diagnosed. At this point she said she felt fine but remained flat with legs elevated at my insistence, until rescue arrived. She was indeed fine with a normal EKG and was released to go home. I suggested she get further cardiology workup and clearance before trying exercise again.

The oddest thing in retrospect is that I did not hesitate or stop to consider my nine months on the sideline. I was Pavlov's dog answering the dinner bell. It was purely reflex. It was what I do—or did. And it felt good to be of use in this manner, to stabilize an unstable emergent situation, to analyze a very human problem, to do what doctors do every day. I'd forgotten how good it feels. Not good enough to reopen my practice but pretty darned good.

JUST FOR FUN

HOW NOT TO IMPRESS A DATE

1. Don't ignore the first adjective in the name of the group which brought you together, For example: *J*-Date or *Christian* Singles. If you are Buddhist or a card carrying member of Satan's disciples, perhaps it's best to start elsewhere.

2. Girls: Don't submit Scarlett Johansson's photo as your own. Even allowing for aging and a few pounds of weight gain, he will figure it out pretty quickly and your future credibility will be shot. Same for guys: Remember it is highly unlikely that random luck will have produced a Ryan Gosling look-alike, especially if your only association with a six pack is bought at the Quik Stop.

3. Guys, don't list your income as "Seven Figures" if you drive a 1998 Dodge Dart.

4. Ladies, avoid the phrase "full figured", "Rubinesque", and "good personality." Maybe it's best to go with the Scarlett Johansson photo and talk quickly before he says, "Taxi!"

5. Be yourself, except if that includes dribbling soup on everything south of your mouth. You might consider toning down, just a bit, whatever grossed out your last date.

6. Don't bring her home after the first date if you live with your mother, unless Mom has been prewarned, takes out the rollers and carries her quart bottle of 'Two Buck Chuck' to her room.

7. Listen, listen, listen. Everyone wants to be heard. How can you expect her to be impressed with your bowling score if you haven't asked about her prison tattoos?

Whatever you do, don't tell your date you are an unpublished writer. That is the same as saying you are virginal gigolo or eunuch with plans for a large family. Even Ryan Gosling couldn't get away with that one!

HOW DO YOU KNOW?

Observations made after going to the gym:
How do you know when others are getting older?
More important, how do you know when others see you
as aging?

1. At the gym the only people with their shirts
    tucked in are over 65. This is more of a tell-
    tale than gray hair or a limp which hint at age
    or retirement but can have other explanations.
    People gray prematurely and some men welcome
    the gravitas that accompanies a few gray hairs.
    Weekend athletes, especially those of middle
    years are known to have Monday morning or-
    thopedic visits leading to physical therapy at the

gym. A tucked in shirt is like wearing a sign saying, "Proud Member of AARP since 1985."

2. If you participate in pool aerobics there is a 99% chance the government sends you a Social Security check each month.

3. If you wear briefs and not boxers (men only) you've been labeled. With women it's trickier since they have adopted men's briefs like they have men's names (think Leslie, Jordan or Sidney with a "y").

4. If you go to the gym at 10 a.m. and don't look like one of those buff fire rescue guys on the late shift, or a new mother trying to reconstitute her waistline, it is likely you are retired.

5. If you have flaming red hair in a color Mother Nature never imagined and use the recumbent bike you've been busted. See #1 re: hair color.

6. If you use the recumbent bike period—it is easy on backs and still provides controlled amounts of resistance to the legs and hips while increasing the heart rate. You can also read while on it! This allows you to appear intellectual while studying to get your driver's license back.

7. If you ask for a senior discount for Gatorade, or club membership or park in a disabled spot using a disability sticker obtained years ago when your spouse tripped over your sneakers when

going to the bathroom at night, you are undeniably labeled.

8. If you use the gym equipment incorrectly then spend inordinate amounts of time bending to within two inches of the instructions since you didn't take your reading glasses to the gym (who knew you would need them!), and walk away mumbling that the damned thing is broken then even the passersby on the street know.

9. If you wear black socks with your Keds and plaid shorts and bring an umbrella every day, even when there is not a cloud for a hundred miles in any direction....then you know.

10. If you don't go because of all of the above or other nonsense excuses because really, who cares how others label you. Each person walking into that gym has concerns. Some are obsessed with body image; some trying to get something back; some worrying about what they are not doing during the time they are in the gym.

In 38 years of medical practice I never once found someone who was entirely happy with their body. Not once!

So my advice to seniors is to focus on the good that exercise does for your body and disregard what you think others are thinking. Most are too busy looking in the mirrors or checking their heart rates to dwell on your issues. Enjoy the workout and watch CNBC. You might learn how to make your IRA last longer.

I GREW A BEARD

I grew a beard. It was a new me. Not a full rabbinical variety. Not a ZZ Top look-alike. Not a presumptuous soul beard implying coolness that I could not hope to possess. It was a conservative well-defined goatee, manly, even professorial. It radiated professional status and confidence, saying here is a serious man of consequence with a hint of style, dare I say hipness, a lover of Jazz.

It itched a little, just enough for me to stroke (and secretly scratch), projecting not just thinking but deep thought; a man considering profound paradoxes of the universe. I mulled over buying a tweed sport jacket with leather elbow patches. Pipe smoking was out of the question and an ascot was pretentious to the extreme. What about an Afghan hound? Too much commitment.

What if next year a pencil thin moustache appealed? My daughter would not easily accept a fourth dog.

It hid a small rash that was forming beneath it. Putting medicinal cream through the hair became problematic. Hygiene was not an issue as I compulsively checked in a mirror after using a tissue, for residual paper or whatever. There was the nose hair conundrum. Does having adjacent hair over ones lip give nasal hair a license to grow freely and uncut. After thorough consideration I decided to wait a few more weeks until it became noticeable and see how this growth affected the whole look. Gross would clearly subtract from substantial, but that was an issue for another day.

So far there were no complaints from my family about the feel with kissing. Hugging and roughhousing with the grandchildren were met with the usual giggling and not complaints of beard abrasion.

Fact is no one noticed.

After waiting endlessly for comments, I would point out my new image defining growth. The response was, "Oh," not, "Wow," or "You look so…." Just a space filling, nonplussed, "Oh."

Far worse than disagreement or even repulsion is not being noticed. How can my new persona be a wallflower, part of the scenery? I was going for, "Why you look terrific," not, "Why bother?"

Today I shaved.

I wonder what a ponytail says?

THINGS THAT MAKE ME HAPPY

Hearing my wife Marilyn sing along with a TV show. Seeing anything that my granddaughter Maia creates.

Hearing about accomplishments of my grandsons, be they school plays, tennis team, good grades, the latest softball excitement, or college adventure.

Hearing from my children. Spending time with my children and grandchildren.

Knowing that we have such good friends in this world.

With earphones on and the TV sound off, hearing Marilyn answer the Jeopardy questions faster than the contestants.

Linguini malafemina (lobster, shrimp, clam, mussels, fish) at *Romanza* restaurant.

Writing Class. The people are spectacularly honest, cheerful and it is a pleasure to share their work and their lives.

The recumbent bike at the *YMCA.*

Reading on said recumbent bike.

Making M laugh.

Being busy.

Being able to help the kids should they need it.

Driving.

Writing.

Sleeping late as I want.

Breakfast at *Lots of Lox.*

Family vacations especially if they include a talent show.

The next big thing, as long as I'm not in charge.

Asheville.

NON-SENSE

"Can't you smell that rotten odor?" asks my wife. To which I answer, "No."

"How do you like the smell of that barbeque?" asks my brother-in-law. "What smell?" I respond. "How can you not smell that?" My reply: "Would you ask a blind man how he cannot see that gorgeous sunset?"

I have not been able to smell for well over ten years. It came upon me gradually, almost unnoticed in its arrival. Eventually anosmia, as it is known, persisted for all but brief interludes, when I would notice a familiar smell or taste. Yes taste, for much of it is derived from smell; salt and sweet persist; food textures and temperature still make foods discernible. The result is a blunting of flavor that leads to the use of more spices, especially hot sauce on eggs, or meats or veggies. In the south there are contests to see who can eat the hottest peppers. I'll bet that most of the contestants have anosmia.

One would think that the loss of smell would lead to weight loss, but in some cases it is the opposite. Satiety shifts from smell and /or taste to a sense of fullness or often over-fullness. The act of eating, and the attendant social aspects of a meal with others, are still very pleasant, though the scent and flavor of food is like a pastel sunset behind thin clouds.

I have gone down the medical trail to a dead end, all tests being normal including the MRI which did not show anything ominous pressing on my olfactory nerves. The ENT doctor says that this condition often follows head trauma. About fifteen years ago I did have my brain shaken like a bowl of jelly when the rear end of my car was struck at forty miles an hour as I waited for a traffic light to change. The eighteen-year-old driver was looking at her beeper instead of my bumper and never even hit the brake as she relocated the trunk of my car into the back seat. I looked at the policeman as if he were speaking French. My son had to make all the decisions. For three days I could not concentrate nor understand many simple conversations, leading to a self diagnosis of concussion—apparently with sufficient brain rock and roll to eventually disrupt one of my favorite senses.

It's not all bad, because I am impervious to sweat sock smells, and Mount Trashmore, and even my grandson's gas, which has been known to clear the front section of a movie theater. Cooking Brussel sprouts does not upset me, though peeling onions will still lead to tears.

There is the safety issue of not recognizing noxious fumes or even smoke. For these I depend on my wife who could make the average bloodhound seem to have nasal stuffiness. I am aware of one sense overcompensating for the loss of another, but I've never seen the compensation occur in the spouse of the nasally challenged. The knowledge that my wife could smell the slightest molecule of perfume on my presence has ensured that I have kept other women at arm's length for the past forty-nine years. It appears a stretch to credit a long happy marriage to her sense of smell and my lack of same; but as a relative once said, "a little paranoia is good for a relationship."

I do miss not having a sense of smell, but less than you might imagine. In most situations I am not unhappy with the status quo. I guess the test is to ask what I would trade to be able to smell: certainly not sight, or hearing, or touch. I could live long and well not being able to tell Coke from Pepsi, or even lamb-burgers from hamburgers. All we are missing is a consciousness raising anosmia support group with a catchy name. I'm partial to a name suggested by *Robert's Rules*: "Call to Odor."

ON MEMORY

Everyone I know is memory obsessed, viewing the word or name they cannot recall as a window into their future, seeing images of progressive neurologic deterioration, loss of independence and dribbling down one's bib. That eminent neurophysiologist Dave Barry claims that at age sixty-five, "the noun center shrivels up like a raisin." Judith Viorst offers a practical mantra when recall fails: "I knew it before, I'll know it again, I just don't know it right now." My wife has created a test to reassure her when she can't come up with, "the actress, who was in that movie, with the guy with the hair...." She must name three performers who have escaped remembrance in the past: Gene Hackman, Christopher Walken, and Phil Collins. If the elusive three can be recalled before anxiety sets in, then all is stable.

I submit that the problem is merely one of traffic control and volume, as if our brains were US1 in 1960 compared with the same road today.

The slow routing of impulses through the brain's hippocampus is one cause of recall delay; no less than one slow light can clog an entire highway. The name *Hippocampus* suggests a wide highway over which requests for information are filled from the library of stored images that is our memory. The ruts in this highway accumulate, as do the years. By age seventy the information, though present, plays hard to get when needed, picking its way around the damaged section of memory lane. The obvious solution is to allow an appropriate amount of time to cross this obstruction—say twenty-four hours. Give yourself permission to wait unstressed for a full day and more often than not, the answer will materialize in the next thirty minutes.

There is the added congestion caused by the sheer volume of information required of a seventy-year-old brain. In the twenties there were friends and relatives and their spouses or dates to remember. Now, they have wed, reproduced, and that generation also has progeny. So now you have to keep straight the original ten friends and relatives, who have a total of twenty-seven children, forty-nine grandchildren (and more on the way), thirty-two pets, (each of which has a name and back story) not to mention jobs, housing issues and in-law conflicts,

A real friend also has to be aware of the health status of their peers; which hip was replaced and when; who is going in for which procedure (colonoscopy, arthroscopy, this or that biopsy, physical therapy) and even who is up all night caring for someone else with these ailments. It can get quite technical, especially if you recall a friend's liver function tests as slightly elevated, when in fact they are rising to alarming levels and you are clueless as to where the second opinion will be sought.

Cheat sheets can be helpful, as is a wife who spends hours a day on the phone commiserating with the one whose turn it is to max out all Medicare deductibles and co-pays.

Where is Google when we really need it? Wouldn't it be of more help to look up Cousin Marc with a c and get his whole bio, name of kids, pets, illnesses and which gift he gave on the last visit—so you can pull it out of the Good Will pile in the garage? You could also do a quick cram before the family get together and hope your recent memory can outlast the greetings at the front door.

Til then, there's always Gene Hackman, Phil Collins and what's his name with the weird hair.

MEMORY HELP!

I find myself pre-empting memory issues by creating ever more complex reminders. In days past a note written on the palm would suffice. These days my palm is not big enough. I'd start looking like one of those guys with entire Bible verses tattooed up their arms and necks. There was always the string tied around your finger, which created the anxiety of something forgotten without the specificity of a reminder.

As a half measure I began putting things in my path so I would literally trip over them on the way to the bathroom or car—hoping of course I could separate the reasons for going to each. Then I heard about a friend who did trip and injure herself, so the obstacle approach to memory was canned.

Pills, ever a challenge to remember, as in "Did I or didn't I take...?" resulted in the glass half-full trick. I would get up and before I would wash my face, I half filled the water cup. Later when pill time rolled around, that water level signaled that I needed to take my pills; an empty cup meant the opposite. It worked most of the time, except occasionally there was a great rerun of Jon Stewart or Colbert (Steven, you will be sorely missed, truthinessly) which made me race into the bedroom homing in on the sounds of my wife's laughter—and you guessed it, forgetting to fill or empty the cup. Then the choice was to under or overdose. I always chose the former, not feeling bad because I was usually still laughing at the common sense revealed by my favorite TV duo as they skewered the pompous and powerful.

My belt is at times filled with displaced items needing to find their homes. There is the garage door opener, which should have been replaced in the car two days ago. There is the pedometer which needs to be transferred to the gym shorts so it can record half (!) of the revolutions of the stationary bike pedals. (How will I ever get to 10,000?) The belt itself doubles as a reminder when I pull it one notch too tight to remind me to have my suit pants let out so they can accommodate the dessert buffet.

There are the "to do lists", part of my *e-solution*, typed into the *notes* app of my i-phone. This sounds so tech savvy doesn't it, well don't be fooled: it's just another attic to store stuff out of sight and out of mind. There are the notes on the desk, "see 'to do' list, on i-phone", the post-it on the door to look at the note on the desk …. The chain of hints sometimes seems like a scavenger hunt.

Like all things, the reminders are good in moderation. They serve a positive function for me by emphasizing how wonderful it is when the name of that restaurant, with the great linguini malafemmina, pops into your mind from some unseen reservoir you knew was there all the time, not to mention Gene Hackman, Christoper Walken and Phil Collins.*

* (See previous essay "On Memory." You remember that one, don't you?)

COME IN

The old Borscht Circuit joke has become reality. "My health is good, knock wood." (He wraps his knuckles on the table twice, then turns to the door.) *"Come in."*

The "come in" moments are becoming more frequent as we enter the down side of our seventh decade; let's just say our late, late sixties.

So last night at dinner, my friend Henry was extolling the virtues of *Innocent*, the follow-up best seller to *Presumed Innocent*, both made into blockbuster movies starring Harrison Ford. He was re-reading *Innocent* because he couldn't remember all the plot twists. I suspect he picked it up not remembering he had read it at all, and then continued to read as it continued to surprise. So Marilyn said, "We just got *Identical* on our Kindle by

Scott Turow." "Hmm," said Henry. "What else did he write?" (1) *"Come in."*

Another friend Dave was in the shower and needed a towel. Wet and cold he yelled for his wife to get him a towel from the dryer. She came in and said "What are you yelling about?" "There's never a towel when I need one!" "It's around your waist," she replied. *"Come in."*

Being precocious, my own moment came thirty years ago when on vacation in Marco Island. As sometimes happens I awakened just as the sun was rising and decided to go for a walk. After dressing and sneaking out as noiselessly as possible, I walked randomly as the predawn mist became streaked with orange. So if I were stranded on an island could I figure out the geography of the world just using logic? I began with the direction of the sunrise and mapped the Island, all of South Florida and the rest of the world, which followed easily.

An hour later I encountered my first pedestrian. Bursting with a need to demonstrate my geographic prowess, I pointed with pride and said "Tampa's that way, right?" "No," he said, pointing in the opposite direction. "But how is that possible if Miami is that way?" I said, pointing to my home city on the map in my head and getting a bit more agitated. "No, Miami is there," he said, pointing opposite and taking a few steps backward while planning his escape from this disoriented and potentially dangerous individual. "But how is that possible?" I said indignantly, sensing that the stranger was pulling a cruel prank. I had figured it all out.... With perfect logic.... From first principles. I would have to prove it to him.

"Look," I said patiently, "If the sun rises in the west..." *"Come in."*

The good thing is we can still laugh about it. Knock wood.

1. Scott Turow is the author of Innocent and Presumed Innocent

PARTY ON

In three months I will be seventy years old. Oops, I forgot the!

So how to deal with this tragic-fortunate-joyous event? First is the recognition of conflicting feelings. I am overjoyed to be passing the milestone that eluded nearly all of my antecedents. None, not one, made it to seventy-one, only two to age seventy, most exiting in their early sixties or fifties. Not that I take any credit, for I did nothing more than swallow two pills a day, one for blood pressure and a statin for cholesterol, while downing more than my share of brisket and chopped liver .

Why tragic? Well yikes! I'm older than Grandpa Harry, a short gray-haired man who sat bent over *The Forward* in the tiny Brooklyn apartment that magically expanded on Passover to accommodate the families of four daughters. I've lived longer than Jackie Robinson, Roy Campanella and Gil Hodges, whose pictures from the World Series winning 1955 Brooklyn Dodgers stare at me across my desk.

My recreation now includes canasta and going nowhere on a stationary bike, instead of Colorado skiing and Cayman Island scuba diving. My days are no longer organized around an office, unless you consider the multiple doctors' offices, where I now sit on the other side of the desk and their (uggghhhhh), computers.

To celebrate or ignore it all, that is the question. Since I'm a big list maker when it comes to decisions, I'll share this one with you.

AGAINST:

Am I inconveniencing everyone and creating an expense for some—airfare, hotels etc?

School vacations for my two sets of grandchildren don't jibe.

I don't enjoy being the center of attention. Opening presents with everyone watching is a special form of torture.

FOR:

Milestones are memories.
It will be great to see everyone together.

Family and friends have asked about it.
It's a PARTY!

I have seen others invoke mystic concepts when it comes to big anniversaries or birthdays, such as the "evil eye" bringing bad fortune upon yourself if you celebrate i.e. brag about your good fortune. They cite someone they knew who had a blowout 50th anniversary celebration and then—fill in the tragedy. They try to sneak over the threshold unnoticed by the forces of karma.

I've often said that if a tragedy waits, that is a reason *to have* a party, not to avoid one. So the decision is clear. To quote *Bill and Ted's Excellent Adventure*: "Party on Dudes."

I'll let you all know where it will be when I find out whose parents will be away for the weekend.

MY PSYCHIATRIST

I would like to thank my psychiatrist, Dr. Qwerty, who was always in, no appointment necessary. Just power up, sidle over and share—share the wordplay, the thought that lingered from the early morning dream, the image that ended a night's rest. He absorbed without judgment. Feelings of weakness or unworthy worries shared with him alone, his expression unchanged. He confronted me with my own words, forcing me to re-examine. I cannot deny what I have pounded into print. I stand accused by my own deficiencies—delineated and organized in double spaced confession. Yet he handed down no verdicts.

Storm clouds gathered and were recorded. Admissions were made, sharing done of a most intimate nature. And there were jokes, good jokes enjoyed by only one, for not even a hint of a grin stained his visage. What a stoic!

How could this one-sided exchange be of benefit? But it clearly is. The worry migrates down my arms to tense fingers, to keyboard, to screen no less surely than electricity travels in a wire. The resulting shock at visualizing the welled-up emotion is palpable. Then there is the predictable wave of relief, not just for cleverly arranging words but also for the quantum shift of negative energy from patient to therapist. My spirit restored and sole uplifted, I am enlightened by the insights which should have been so obvious.

He accepts no insurance but his rates are the most reasonable in town and he is worth so much more!

He has his methods, Dr. Qwerty. Maybe not warm and fuzzy but effective every time.

P aul M. Gustman, MD, grew up in a financially challenged family in Brooklyn, New York, before attending and interning at the Medical College of Virginia. He went on to practice pulmonary medicine and critical care for thirty-eight years in Miami, Florida.

After retiring in 2013, Dr. Gustman began studying writing at the Osher Lifelong Learning Institute at the University of Miami and is now an award-winning essayist.

He has been married to his wife, Marilyn, for forty-nine years and is the father of two and grandfather of six.

CPSIA information can be obtained
at www.ICGtesting.com
Printed in the USA
LVOW04s2344160316
479502LV00024B/509/P